Filing for Chapter 7 Bankruptcy

Bankruptcy

What You Need to Know

Christopher M. Kennedy

Project Manager, Kristen Lindeman; edited by Jo Alice Darden, proofread by Melanie Zimmerman

ISBN 978-0-314-27492-2

For corrections, updates, comments, or any other inquiries, please e-mail
TLR.AspatoreEditorial@thomson.com.

First Printing, 2011
10 9 8 7 6 5 4 3 2 1

Mat #41127500

DEDICATION

I want to thank my family for their support and patience.

CONTENTS

Introduction

Bankruptcy. There may not be a scarier word in the English language. The mere word conjures up images of destitution and failure. There is a feeling that someone is getting away with something. Many of these images are shaped by the bankruptcies that make the news, corporations, sports stars, and newsmakers. The perception is that the bankruptcy was caused by greed, corruption, or mismanagement. Certainly, this image is reinforced by the high-profile bankruptcies of rappers and sports stars. Cases where the image is a life of excess and failure to anticipate a future with lower earnings lead to the inevitable bankruptcy filing.

The truth of the matter is that those cases are rare. Most bankruptcies are by individuals who can be your friends, neighbors, or relatives. These bankruptcies are not caused by living the high life at the expense of your creditors, but rather a traumatic change of circumstances. This may be an illness in which insurance did not pay, the loss of a job, or the failure of a business. These unexpected changes of circumstances lead many people to seek the relief offered in the bankruptcy code.

1

History of Bankruptcy

As with many legal concepts, we can trace elements of bankruptcy or debt forgiveness to various cultures. In biblical times, there was the practice of a Jubilee, or holy year that was to take place every fifty years. One of the provisions of the Jubilee was the elimination of debts. This was not the case in other ancient cultures. In ancient Greece, if a man owed a debt and was unable to pay, his family, including servants, became debt slaves.

Our system of bankruptcy has its roots in England. The first official laws on bankruptcy were passed in 1542 during the reign of Henry VIII. This law allowed for the imprisonment of debtors for the failure to pay debts and was the historical beginning of debtor's prisons. This Dickensonian version of debt provided that if you were not able to pay your debt, you would be placed in prison until you were able to pay. As the result of the inequities of these laws, in the early 1700s came the first laws to introduce the idea that there should be a discharge of an unpaid debt. The laws limited the circumstances in which this could occur, but it marked the beginning of the acceptance of the concept that the law should protect the debtor.

Our founding fathers addressed the issue of bankruptcy in the Constitution. Article 1, Section 8 of the United States Constitution authorizes Congress to enact uniform laws on the subject of bankruptcy. This constitutional provision has provided the basis for a federal system of bankruptcy, rather than a state-by-state system. Under this grant of authority, Congress has enacted several bankruptcy laws.

Early bankruptcy laws in the United States followed the English concepts of debtors and creditors and were enacted in response to specific economic conditions. The first official bankruptcy law was enacted in 1800 in response to rampant land speculation. The law was later repealed. In 1837, a bankruptcy law was passed in response to a panic. This law was repealed in 1843. Another bankruptcy law was passed in 1867. That law was repealed in 1878. All of these laws allowed for the discharge of some debts, though the protections provided to debtors would be minimal by today's standards. All the early American attempts at bankruptcy regulation greatly favored creditors. This led to a system where the majority of bankruptcies were brought by the creditors and not the debtor. The focus of the laws was on the creditors and recovery of a portion of their debts.

The Bankruptcy Act of 1898 was the first law that was enacted that we are able to consider a modern bankruptcy law. In this act, the focus of the bankruptcy shifted from punishing the debtor and paying the creditors to reorganizing the debtor in distress. This played a crucial role for corporations, as it provided protection from creditors that would allow a business to continue to operate. Previously, many businesses had to be liquidated to pay their debts.

The United States overhauled bankruptcy laws in 1938. This included the creation of Chapter 13. There was another major overhaul in 1978. One of the aims of the changes was to encourage the greater use of Chapter 13. This would be similar to one of the goals of the reforms of the revisions in 2005. In practice, the provisions under the law did not meet the goal, and for many, Chapter 7 remained the option that was the most attractive. The 2005 revisions were made because of concerns of Congress and others that those debtors were taking advantage of the bankruptcy code for nefarious reasons. The reforms include the requirement that individuals take classes both prior to filing and after they have filed, but before receiving a discharge and the means test.

The Bankruptcy Code of 1978 with revisions remains the law of the land.

2

Bankruptcy Basics

Bankruptcy is a process to provide the honest but unfortunate debtor a fresh start. This is a well-known axiom that provides a basis for what bankruptcy means for a debtor. As expressed by the US Supreme Court, it is the purpose of bankruptcy to give an honest but unfortunate debtor a new opportunity in life, unfettered by the pressure and burdens of the previous debts. *Local Loan Company v. Hunt*, 292 US 234, 244 (1934). It is one of the core principles of the bankruptcy process.

The Bankruptcy Code is still the uniform federal law that governs all bankruptcy cases. In addition, bankruptcy cases are governed by the Bankruptcy Rules of Procedure and the local rules of the bankruptcy courts. The Bankruptcy Rules and local rules of the bankruptcy courts provide the forms that are used in filing the bankruptcy.

The local rules are created by the individual judicial district. There is at least one district in every state. Many states have multiple districts. Now there are ninety districts in the United States. Each of the districts has its own local rules. These rules, along with the Bankruptcy Rules of Procedure and the Bankruptcy Code, will govern how a particular bankruptcy is handled.

The Process of Bankruptcy

A number of persons are involved in any bankruptcy case. The court official with decision-making power is the US bankruptcy judge. The bankruptcy judge is a judicial officer with US district court. The bankruptcy judge will decide any contested matter in the bankruptcy. This will include issues such as the debtor's eligibility to file, whether the debtor should receive a discharge of all debts, whether a certain debt may be discharged, and whether an asset is exempt or remains property of the bankruptcy, to name a few. In these cases, a party in interest will file a complaint that will start an adversary proceeding. This is a similar process to the commencement of a lawsuit. In a typical case a Chapter 7 debtor will not have to appear before a judge, and a Chapter 13 debtor may have to appear only once at the hearing to confirm the repayment plan. (See below for an explanation of filing types.)

In most cases, a bankruptcy will be primarily an administrative process that is conducted away from the courthouse. The bankruptcy petition and schedules will be filed, and the case will be assigned to a trustee. The bankruptcy trustee is the person who will oversee the bankruptcy and will attempt to find assets for the bankruptcy estate. It is the trustee's job to review the petition and schedules, determine whether any assets remain in the bankruptcy estate, and whether to liquidate those assets and distribute the funds to the creditors.

The only required hearing will be the meeting of creditors, which is also referred to as the Section 341 hearing—a reference to the Bankruptcy Code section that requires the debtor's attendance at this hearing. While the hearing is referred to as the Meeting of Creditors, in most cases, no creditors appear. At the hearing, the trustee is required to verify the identity of the debtor, as well as the debtor's Social Security number. In addition, the trustee will ask questions to verify the information in the bankruptcy petition and schedules.

Types of Filings

The Bankruptcy Code provides for six different types of bankruptcy. Bankruptcies are referred to by the chapter number that authorizes their use. For example, when we use the term Chapter 7, we are referring to the bankruptcy provided for under Chapter 7 of the Bankruptcy Code.

Chapter 7 bankruptcy is provided for under 11 US Code Chapter 7, and is referred to as a liquidation or fresh start. Chapter 7 contemplates an orderly, supervised procedure by which the bankruptcy trustee takes over the assets of the debtor's estate and reduces those assets to cash. These funds are then used to pay creditors proportionate shares of any claims they may have.

The debtor's estate includes not only assets that are owned by the debtor on the date of filing, but also the ability of the trustee to go after preferential payments. If an individual or a couple files the Chapter 7 bankruptcy petition, they are provided laws referred to as exemptions that will allow them to protect certain property. This will allow them the fresh start without the need to incur new debt to provide for necessities. These exemptions vary by state but include the ability to protect some equity in a home, household goods and furnishings, and some equity in a motor vehicle.

After the debtor claims his or her exemptions, there may be no property left in the bankruptcy estate. These cases are termed no-asset cases. In asset cases, a creditor will be required to file a proof of claim. Creditors who fail to file proofs of claim will not receive their portions of the distribution.

A few months after the debtor files for bankruptcy protection, he or she will receive a discharge, which is the court order barring creditors from being able to collect on their debts.

Chapter 7 bankruptcy was revised with new provisions in 2005. This includes a requirement that the debtor take two classes and a requirement for the application of a "means test." One class is required before the debtor can file bankruptcy; the class covers the options under the Bankruptcy Code and outside of the Bankruptcy Code to deal with debts. The debtor's second class concerns financial management—how to manage finances. The "means test" refers to an application that is made as part of the bankruptcy petition. The test compares the debtor's income to the mean income for the bankruptcy district where he or she resides. If the income is higher than that amount, the presumption is that they do not qualify for Chapter 7, but rather should be filing for relief under Chapter 13.

Chapter 13 is designed for the adjustment of debts of an individual with a source of regular income. Chapter 13 is sometimes preferable to Chapter 7. It allows a debtor to keep his or her property as long as the payments in the plan are more than the value of the non-exempt assets.

The debtor prepares a plan to repay creditors over time. This is generally done over three to five years. Chapter 13 is also for individuals who fail the means tests. The debtor will propose a repayment plan, and then the bankruptcy court at a confirmation hearing will either accept or deny the plan, based on whether it complies with the Bankruptcy Code's requirements for confirmation. In most cases, the debtor will remain in possession of the property of the estate. The payments are made to the Chapter 13 trustee, who will make the payments to the creditors. The debtor will not receive a discharge in the bankruptcy immediately; rather, the plan will have to be completed before the debtor receives that relief. During the bankruptcy, the debtor is protected from collection actions and lawsuits from most unsecured creditors. The debts that are discharged in a Chapter 13 bankruptcy are also broader than those in a Chapter 7.

A debtor filing for Chapter 11 bankruptcy is entitled to reorganization. Corporations generally use it, though on occasion individuals who would not otherwise qualify for Chapter 13 use it, as well.

The Chapter 11 debtor files a petition and schedules with the court and has 120 days after it files to propose a plan of reorganization. The debtor must provide the creditors with a statement that gives the creditor enough information to review the plan. The creditor then has an opportunity to take action if needed.

The bankruptcy court will approve or disapprove of the plan of reorganization. The plan may allow a debtor to reduce its obligations by repayment of a portion of the previous debts. The debtor may be able to discharge other obligations and can accept or reject contracts and leases, recover assets, and revise the corporation to return it to profitability.

Chapter 12 is called Adjustment of Debts of a Family Farmer or Fisherman with a Regular Annual Income. The process of a Chapter 12 bankruptcy is similar to the process under Chapter 13. The debtor proposes a plan to repay debts over a period. The plan is limited to three years unless the court approves a longer period, but in no case can it be more than five years. While similar to a Chapter 13, the Chapter 12 bankruptcy is modified to help the family farmer or angler to obtain bankruptcy relief.

Chapter 9 is titled Adjustment of Debts of a Municipality. These are uncommon, but it is necessary to recognize that governmental entities are not able to reorganize in the manner of other debtors. This provision is limited to cities, towns, villages, counties, tax districts, municipal utilities, and school districts. The chapter provides a manner in which these creditors can reorganize.

Chapter 15 is called the Ancillary and Other Cross Boarder Insolvency. The purpose is an attempt to ease the issues that are raised when a debtor or the debtor's property is subject to the laws of the United States and one or more foreign jurisdictions.

3

Who Should File for Bankruptcy?

Bankruptcy is meant to be a safety net. It is there to protect persons and entities that have found themselves in financial situations they just cannot get themselves out of. It is also there for the business that needs help to reorganize or wind up its affairs.

A business should consider filing for bankruptcy protection if the action is necessary to protect assets from the collection efforts of creditors—in particular if those collection efforts will result in the end of the business. Reorganization will provide the business with time to address the issues of the creditors. If the business cannot be saved, the bankruptcy will provide a method by which to wind up the affairs of the business.

It is more difficult for an individual or couple to make the decision to file. A person should consider the amount of his or her debt, the type of debt, whether that debt can be discharged in bankruptcy, and the length of time it will take to repay the debt. The individual must compare this with his or her income. If he or she cannot pay the debt off in a reasonable time period—five to ten years—bankruptcy may still be an option.

In some cases, bankruptcy is appropriate to save a home. If the debtor is behind in payments and the home has not been sold at a sheriff's sale, Chapter 13 bankruptcy has provisions that would allow the debtor to reinstate the mortgage payments. This requires the debtor to make a payment and then a second payment to the bankruptcy plan.

In some cases, bankruptcy is filed to prevent the garnishment of wages or to prevent creditors from taking property. The bankruptcy will have the automatic stay that will prevent creditors from taking action to collect on debts.

4

Who Can File for Chapter 7 Bankruptcy Relief?

To qualify to file for protection under Chapter 7 of the Bankruptcy Code, you must be an individual, a married couple, a corporation, a limited liability corporation, or a limited liability partnership. Chapter 7 bankruptcy is not limited only to individuals. If you are married, there is no requirement that you and your spouse both file; it is permissible for one spouse to file and not the other. In some cases, this may make sense, such as if the debt is primarily credit card debt that was incurred by you and not your spouse. Often, the debt is a joint obligation, and a joint bankruptcy filing is more practical. This is particularly true in cases where there is significant medical debt, as many states make this an obligation of the spouse, even if the spouse did not sign any agreement.

There is no debt limit or floor. There is not even a requirement that you be insolvent. In many ways, it is easier to state who cannot file for Chapter 7 bankruptcy protection. You cannot file for Chapter 7 bankruptcy protection if, during the 180 days prior to the bankruptcy filing, you filed a bankruptcy petition that was dismissed because of your willful failure to appear before the court or to comply with a court order. You will also be barred if a previous case was voluntarily dismissed after a creditor had requested that the court grant permission for it to recover property on which it had a secured interest. You may ask, why would somebody file for bankruptcy, voluntarily dismiss the case, and then re-file. This is a common practice to prevent foreclosure. The bank or other secured lender would start the foreclosure process, the debtor would file a bankruptcy petition, the secured party would seek permission for the Court to go forward with the foreclosure, the debtor would dismiss the bankruptcy, and the debtor would then file another bankruptcy. The purpose was to obtain the protection of the Bankruptcy Automatic Stay and to maintain the property for as long as possible.

If you have previously filed a Chapter 7 bankruptcy and were granted a discharge in the past eight years, you do not qualify to file again within that eight year time period. In addition, if you have received a discharge in a Chapter 13 bankruptcy that was filed in the past six years, you will not be granted a discharge unless you paid your unsecured claims more than 70 percent of the amount due.

In order to file, you will be required to have completed credit counseling within 180 days of the filing date. Credit counseling is a requirement put in place by the bankruptcy reforms of 2005. Congress made this requirement with the intention of providing additional information to debtors before they file. The class is meant to provide information so that you, the debtor, are fully informed of all the options. Except in limited circumstances, such as being on active duty in the military, or when the bankruptcy district does not have an approved provider, this requirement is absolute. This means you must take the class and have the certificate before you can file. If you take the class and the bankruptcy filing is delayed, it may be possible that you will have to take the class a second time. The certificates are no good after 180 days. The class must be provided by an approved credit-counseling provider. Generally, you may find a list of the approved providers at the website for the bankruptcy court of the district in which you file. If you do not take the class and file a certificate with the court, your case will be dismissed, and you will lose the filing fee.

Eligibility to file a Chapter 7 bankruptcy is also subject to your qualifying under the means test. For more information on the means test, see page 23. (Remember to change this after making final revisions.)

5

Why Should I File for Chapter 7?

Filing for bankruptcy should be a difficult decision made only after careful consideration. In some cases, it is the best opportunity for an individual or business to obtain a chance for a fresh start. Once you have made that decision, you must decide which chapter of the bankruptcy code is the best for you.

A Chapter 7 Bankruptcy filing is appropriate for the individual or business that needs to start over. It is appropriate if you do not have many assets and your income is below the median income for your district. It is appropriate for the individual who does not have a regular income and cannot provide regular payments under a Chapter 13 Bankruptcy Plan.

Many times the attraction of the Chapter 7 Bankruptcy is that it is a relatively quick process. You obtain the relief of the Automatic Stay upon filing, meaning that your creditors cannot take actions to collect from you. The bankruptcy estate assets are administered by the bankruptcy trustee, this process may be completed in less than a year. Payments under a Chapter 13 Bankruptcy plan may be made for three to five years. In some cases, all the property you have will be protected by the exemptions that you may claim under state or federal law and the process will be quicker.

A Chapter 7 Bankruptcy is appropriate for individuals who are older, have a number of dependents, income below the median income, and individuals who do not have a regular income. In addition, you will need to have primarily unsecured debts that will be discharged in the bankruptcy. This will be debts such as credit cards and medical bills. It will not be the best choice if you have a high income, are attempting to save your home, have tax debts, or have other debts that will not be discharged in a Chapter 7 case.

In your case, you need to consider the amount of debt that you have. You will need to consider the type of debt that you. You will also have to consider your income. Once you have this information, you can determine whether a bankruptcy is necessary. If you have relatively low debt with a low interest rate, then you may have options other than a bankruptcy. If you have high debts with high interest then the bankruptcy may not be the best option. If you have high debt but it is secured, a bankruptcy may not help. If the debt is unsecured, the bankruptcy may allow you to have a fresh start. This debt should then be considered with your income and expenses. This will show you what you can afford to pay and what you have left to pay the creditors. The longer it will take to pay back the debt the more likely it is that you should file for bankruptcy protection.

6

What Is the Means Test?

The bankruptcy means test was imposed as part of the bankruptcy reforms of 2005. The purpose was to prevent high-earning individuals, who Congress presumed had the ability to pay something to their creditors, from filing for bankruptcy. The means test is the tool Congress implemented to forward this goal. If you fail the means test, you will still be able to file a bankruptcy under Chapter 13, but you will not be able to file under Chapter 7 to wipe out your debts altogether. The means test does not mean you have to be penniless to qualify to file for Chapter 7 bankruptcy; you can have a significant income and still qualify. This is particularly true if you have high expenses from a mortgage or an ongoing medical condition.

To determine whether you pass or fail the means test, you have to determine whether your income is higher or lower than the median income for a family of your size in your state. If your income is lower than the median income, you qualify to file for Chapter 7 bankruptcy protection. For example, if you filed for bankruptcy protection in Minnesota and had a family of four, your income would have to be lower than the median income of $86,329 for you to qualify. If your household income were below this amount, say $75,000, you would qualify to file for Chapter 7 bankruptcy protection. Median income will vary by family size and location. A family of four in Minnesota will have a different median income than a family of four in California.

The analysis becomes more complex if you have an income that is higher than the median income for a family your size in your state. You will have to determine whether you have disposable income—that is, income left over after you have paid your allowed monthly expenses. If you have income left over that would allow you to pay off at least a portion of your unsecured debts, you will fail and will not be able to file for Chapter 7 bankruptcy protection. Just as the median income varies by state, the allowed expenses will vary by metropolitan area or county. A number of online calculators will help with the math.

7

What Happens to My Debts If I File Bankruptcy?

The purpose of filing for Chapter 7 bankruptcy protection is so you can discharge your debts. What this means is that there will be an order from the bankruptcy court that indicates that your creditors are barred from collecting on those debts. This is called a discharge and will be discussed in detail later.

This discharge will apply to most unsecured debts—accounts such as credit cards and medical bills. Secured creditors are protected by the value of the collateral. There are also certain debts that cannot be eliminated in the bankruptcy, such as child support, maintenance, debts incurred by a conviction of driving while intoxicated (DWI), many tax obligations, criminal fines, and debts incurred by fraud.

In the case of secured creditors, you will have to make a choice as to whether or not you want to keep the property that secures the loan. This can be done through a reaffirmation agreement. This is an agreement in which you agree to be responsible for the debt even though you filed bankruptcy. In some cases, you may choose to surrender the property. The creditor will receive the property but any deficiency will be discharged in the bankruptcy. You may also redeem the property, which is a process where you make a lump sum payment to the creditor for the value of the property and the remainder of the debt is discharged.

While many debts that are not discharged are automatically exempted, debts incurred by fraud are not. If a creditor believes that it has a debt that should not be discharged in the bankruptcy, they must bring an adversary action, which is like a lawsuit that is part of the bankruptcy. The Bankruptcy Court will then have to decide if the debt was incurred by fraud and therefore should be exempted by discharge. Any claim of this nature must be filed with the Court within sixty days of the meeting of creditors or the creditor will lose the ability to bring the claim.

8

The Roles and Duties of Major Players in Chapter 7

Duties and Powers of the Trustees

In any bankruptcy, two trustees will each have a role. The attorney general of the United States is required to appoint a US trustee for each of the twenty-one districts in the United States. The role of the US trustee and his or her office is to appoint the Chapter 7 bankruptcy trustees and help with the administration of each case. It is also the role of the US trustee's office to review materials filed by the debtor and provide a statement to the court on whether a presumption of abuse arose. The trustee's office will refer to the US attorney any issues it believes constitute a crime.

It is the role of the Chapter 7 bankruptcy trustee to administer the actual bankruptcy case. The Chapter 7 bankruptcy trustee will ask the questions at the meeting of creditors. He or she will collect any non-exempt property that remains in the bankruptcy estate, liquidate those assets, and then distribute them to the creditors based on the statements of claims filed by the creditors in asset cases. The bankruptcy trustee has to account for and keep records of all of the assets of the bankruptcy estate. The bankruptcy trustee will investigate your financial situation and ensure that you perform your intentions as stated in your Statement of Intention.

The bankruptcy trustee has the power not only to go after assets that are not protected by an available exemption but also to review transfers of property and in some circumstances void those transactions. (This occurs if the transfer was a preferential transfer or it was based on fraud. In a preferential transfer, a payment was made to a creditor for more than it would have received had the payment been made after the bankruptcy filing. Fraudulent transfers are those in which property was sold or transferred for less than full market value.) The purpose of these powers is to ensure that all creditors are treated the same and to prevent unscrupulous debtors from hiding assets or selling assets to friends and family members.

Failure to cooperate with the trustee may lead to the loss of discharge. This means that the trustee will still administer the bankruptcy estate for the benefit of creditors—including selling property that is left in the bankruptcy estate, going after preferential transfers, and making payments to the creditors—but you will not receive a court order barring those creditors from taking further action to collect on their debts. In other words, you will still owe the creditors when the bankruptcy is completed.

Your Duties as a Debtor

When you file for protection of the Bankruptcy Code, you request relief from the court. The specific relief you are requesting is to be discharged from your obligations. To receive that relief, you have a number of duties. Many of these we have already discussed, such as taking the pre-bankruptcy class, taking the post-bankruptcy filing class, meeting the means test, filing a Statement of Intention, and preparing a bankruptcy petition and schedules that accurately reflect your financial situation.

In addition to those duties:

1. You will be required to provide the Chapter 7 bankruptcy trustee copies of your tax returns for the two tax periods prior to your filing at least seven days before the meeting of creditors.

2. You must attend a meeting of creditors and answer the questions of the trustee and the creditors.
3. You must cooperate with the trustee, the US trustee, and the court in the investigation of your case.
4. You must attend any court hearing required by the court.
5. You must surrender the non-exempt property to the bankruptcy trustee.
6. If you receive property or the right to receive property within 180 days after you have filed, you must provide that information to the bankruptcy trustee and the court.
7. You must keep the court informed of your current address.

Failure to perform these duties may lead to the denial of the discharge or the revocation of the discharge if it was previously granted.

Duties of Your Attorney

If you have an attorney, the attorney will be required to help you with the bankruptcy process by:

1. Meeting with you to discuss your financial situation
2. Advising you on the proper bankruptcy chapter, as well as non-bankruptcy options
3. Advising you on the need to provide the bankruptcy trustee with appropriate documents regarding confirming the information in the bankruptcy process
4. Assisting you in the preparation of the bankruptcy petition and schedules
5. Attending with you the meeting of creditors and negotiating with your creditors on any reaffirmation agreements
6. Advising you on any motions that may be filed in the bankruptcy, whether for relief of the automatic stay, objection to exemption, or motion to revoke discharge
7. Advising you on what debts will be discharged and what property will be exempt

9

Documents Required for Filing Chapter 7

To file for bankruptcy, you will need to prepare and file numerous documents with the court that are commonly referred to as the bankruptcy petition and schedules. These documents include:

- Certificate indicating you completed the credit counseling class
- Statement of your pay advices (pay stubs) and copies of any pay stub for the sixty days prior to the filing of the bankruptcy
- Signature Declaration (Declaration of Electronic Filing)
- Bankruptcy Petition
- Summary of Schedules
- Statement of Social Security Number
- Bankruptcy Schedule A: Real Property
- Bankruptcy Schedule B: Personal Property
- Bankruptcy Schedule C: Exempt Property
- Bankruptcy Schedule D: Secured Claims
- Bankruptcy Schedule E: Unsecured Priority Claims
- Bankruptcy Schedule F: Unsecured Claims
- Bankruptcy Schedule G: Executory Contracts and Unexpired Leases
- Bankruptcy Schedule H: Co-debtors
- Bankruptcy Schedule I: Income
- Bankruptcy Schedule J: Expenses
- Declaration Relating to Schedules

- Statement of Intention in Regards to Secured Property
- Statement of Financial Affairs
- Means Test
- Notice to Individual Consumer Debtors

In addition, if you are represented by an attorney, the attorney will file a Statement of Compensation with the court. Various districts may require additional forms—for example, the district of Minnesota requires that all bankruptcy filers file a Statement of Duties with the court, which lists the duties of an attorney and a debtor in a bankruptcy case. The court in which the bankruptcy is being filed should be contacted to determine whether it has additional requirements.

The filing of the petition and schedules with the court will not end the documents you will be required to provide. Once a bankruptcy trustee has been assigned to your case, you will be required to provide the trustee with copies of your taxes for the two most recent tax years. In addition, before you will be able to obtain your discharge, you will be required to take a second credit counseling class on financial management.

It is important that the information in the bankruptcy petition and schedules is accurate, as you are signing the documents under oath. A bankruptcy trustee will ask questions on the information, and at the Section 341 meeting (meeting of creditors), you will have to answer this person's questions under oath. There is also a possibility that the US trustee will audit your case and seek verification of the information contained therein. If you have an attorney, the attorney will also be responsible for that information.

Credit Counseling Certificate

The credit counseling certificate is a document that is not prepared by you, but rather by the credit counseling agency. It certifies to the court that you have completed a course with an approved provider. The cost for this class will vary depending on who provides the class. The requirement for the class was instituted by Congress in 2005 in an effort to educate individuals about their options—the option to file for bankruptcy and options they may have to avoid filing.

A list of approved providers is available from the bankruptcy court for the district in which you file. In addition, the Department of Justice has a list for each district available on its website at www.justice.gov/ust/eo/bacpa/ccde/cc_approved.htm. These classes may be provided in languages other than English.

The class has to be taken by each individual who is filing for bankruptcy protection, so if it is a joint filing, both spouses have to take the class. The only exceptions for not taking the class are having no approved providers for your district or being on active military duty. The class—and, more important, the certificate—are valid for 180 days. In addition to filing the certificate with the court, you will need to prepare and file with the court a statement indicating that you completed the credit counseling.

Consumer Credit Counseling: Financial Management

Financial management is the second class you are required to take as a debtor before you are able to receive your discharge. The purpose of the class is to provide basics about financial management. After you have filed your bankruptcy, but before you receive your discharge, you will have to take this class, obtain a certificate, and file the certificate of completion with the court. The bankruptcy court cannot grant you a discharge until this certificate has been filed.

Statement of Your Payment Advices

The Statement of Payment Advices is required by some jurisdictions, but not all. It is a sworn statement indicating that you have provided the court with copies of all pay stubs you have received in the sixty days leading up to the bankruptcy filing. If you are unemployed, disabled, or self-employed, it will allow you to provide a statement to that effect. You and your spouse will prepare this single form, if necessary. Check with the bankruptcy court to determine whether it is required in your district.

Signature Declaration (Declaration of Electronic Filing)

The signature declaration is a statement that provides the court with notice that you have given your attorney authority to file the bankruptcy petition and schedules electronically. Your signature further indicates that the information being submitted is true and correct. You make this statement under oath. This is a form specific to the various districts, and the precise form may be found with the bankruptcy court.

Bankruptcy Petition

The bankruptcy petition is the basic document that is filed with the court asking for Chapter 7 bankruptcy relief. The form itself is only two pages long and provides the court with the name and address of you and your spouse if you are filing jointly. It will provide the court with notice of the bankruptcy chapter under which you are filing. It has a summary of the information in the schedules, such as a range for the value of the assets and the debts. The petition also provides the court notice of whether you have filed bankruptcy in the past eight years and whether you have taken the credit counseling class.

The information provided in the bankruptcy petition will determine whether you qualify to file and the jurisdiction in which your case needs to be filed. The petition also will request how long you have lived in a jurisdiction, as this may be a factor in determining whether you can file. If you have just moved to a state, you may not qualify to file there. The term of your residence will also determine what exemptions you will be able to use to protect your property.

Summary of Schedules

The Summary of Schedules gives a basic overview of your bankruptcy. If you are using an electronic preparation service or an attorney, you will not need to provide any additional information. The Summary of Schedules provides a brief entry of the totals for each of the Schedules that follow. For example, under Schedule A, the summary will list the value of the real estate you own, and Schedule F will list the amount of all your unsecured debt.

Statement of Social Security Number

The Statement of Social Security Number is just what it says it is—a statement you provide the court of your Social Security number. It is provided in a separate statement because the courts have become concerned that individuals are using the public information in court files to steal identities. The sheet is necessary for the court to verify who you are. The bankruptcy trustee will also verify your Social Security number by a Social Security card or similar document. If you do not have a Social Security number, you will need to apply for one. If you do not qualify for a Social Security number, you will need to apply for a tax identification number.

Bankruptcy Schedules

The bankruptcy schedules are, in essence, the bankruptcy case. It is in these schedules that you will show the court, the trustee, and your creditors your financial circumstances. The schedules will include all your real estate, personal property, and debts. It will also include your income and expenses.

Schedule A: Real Estate

Schedule A provides a complete listing of all property you own or have an ownership interest in, including property you have purchased subject to a mortgage or on a contract for deed. It will also include interest you may have in property by way of a trust or a remainder interest subject to somebody's life estate interest. What is important is that you are able to provide a legal description for the property—the description found in the deed, contract for deed, mortgage, abstract, or Torrens certificate. It may not be the description found in other documents, such as a statement of real estate taxes. It is the legal description that identifies the property— not the property address.

In the bankruptcy process, you will need to provide a basis for the valuation of your property. As with all of the bankruptcy schedules and the information contained in them, you provide this information under oath. If you are unsure of what your property is worth, a good place to search may be the local tax assessment records. Unfortunately, this may not be accurate enough, and you may have to obtain a comparative market analysis from a local realtor. You may have to review the title documents to determine who has what ownership interest in the property.

Schedule B: Personal Property

You will have to provide information on all of the assets you own. This does not mean you have to prepare an inventory of each individual item, but you have to provide enough detail that the trustee has an idea of what property you have. It is important to list your assets properly. The bankruptcy trustee will review them to determine which will remain property of the bankruptcy estate.

This schedule seems to cause people the most confusion and difficulty. While it may be easy to forget an asset, you provide this schedule, like everything else in the bankruptcy case, under oath. False statements in a bankruptcy can lead to a denial of discharge, loss of the asset, or criminal charges. The schedule has thirty-five categories in which to list your assets. The questions are all asked in the same manner—that is, whether you have any property that meets that description of the asset, and if you do, you list the property you have.

1. *Cash:* While this appears to be the simplest question, in fact, it is probably the one most people get wrong—not because the question is difficult, but because people do not think it out. In my practice, when I first ask the question, probably half of my clients will answer "none"; that is rarely a correct answer. Cash means the money in your wallet, purse, change jar, safety deposit box, and sofa cushions. It means any money you have, anywhere in the world.
2. *Checking and Savings Accounts:* This seems to be straightforward, but you may have accounts you do not think of in this manner.

You will have to list all accounts you have with a bank, credit union, or savings and loan institution. You will also have to list any account from which you can withdraw money and in which you have cash. This includes accounts such as PayPal, brokerage accounts with cash balances, and even accounts with online game services. It includes any entity in which you have cash deposited that you can withdraw. For each of these accounts, you will need to provide the balance in the account on day you file.

3. *Security Deposits:* These are the monies you may have on deposit with a landlord or utility service. There are payments you make that are held by a provider to guarantee they will receive payment.

4. *Household Goods and Furnishings:* It may not be necessary to list every knife, fork, and spoon you own, but you will need to provide the trustee a description of your property. You should list electronics, such as large-screen televisions and computers. Valuing this property is difficult for many people; the best value is what you could expect at a conducted house sale, such as an estate sale or auction. If you have items that have a higher value, they should be listed separately.

5. *Books, Pictures, Art Objects, Antiques, and Collectibles:* This is where you list those items that have a higher value. In some cases, you will be able to list a whole collection and provide a value—for example, a stamp, coin, or baseball card collection. In other cases, you should list the specific item. If the items have a high value, they should be listed individually. It is typical for people to use valuations from eBay or auctions to determine the value of their property.

6. *Wearing Apparel:* Generally, this will just be listed as clothing with an overall value, but if you have a designer dress or shoes or antique or vintage clothing, you will need to list these pieces separately.

7. *Furs and Jewelry:* You may list costume jewelry as a collection, but you should list separately any items of significant value. Any item covered by an insurance policy certainly should be listed on its own. Furs should be listed on their own. Valuations on this type of property are always difficult, as it is possible that your

insurance value is significantly over what you paid for a piece. It may be appropriate to take the property to a jeweler or pawnshop to see what it would be willing to pay for the piece.

8. *Firearms, Sporting Goods, Photographic, and Hobby Equipment:* Every gun you have should be listed. In the case of sporting goods, photographic equipment, and hobby goods, it may be possible to list them as a group, but any item with a significant value should be listed by itself.

9. *Insurance Policies:* Many people do not see insurance policies as assets, but they are. In some cases, a whole life policy will have a cash value; this will represent a monetary value to the bankruptcy estate. If you have only term policies, you are still required to list them as assets.

10. *Annuities:* An annuity is a right to receive payment for a specified period. Annuities are common for use in retirement planning or the payment of a personal injury action. If you have an annuity or a right to receive property though an annuity, it is an asset that has to be included in the bankruptcy. You will need to review the annuity contract to determine what interest you have in the annuity. You will also have to consult a discount table to convert that interest into a current market value. In most cases, you should consult an attorney before you file bankruptcy to advise you on what will happen to this asset. If you do not consult with an attorney, you may wish to consult with a financial planner, who can help you evaluate the value of the annuity.

11. *Educational IRA:* You will have to list any education fund you may own, even if the beneficiary is someone other than yourself. Even though this is listed as an education IRA (individual retirement account), you would be required to provide information on any educational account you may have set up for the benefit of yourself or another in which you have an ownership interest.

12. *IRA, Employee Retirement Income Security Act (ERISA), Keogh, or Other Pension Plans:* You will need to list all of your retirement accounts. While the vast majority of these accounts will be protected in the bankruptcy, you are required to list all the

property that you own—not just property that will be property of the bankruptcy estate. This also includes any interest you may have in a retirement account or another pension, such as an interest in a pension fund that was awarded to you as part of dissolution of marriage action.

13. *Stocks and Interests in Businesses:* This category includes shares of any publically traded stock or stock trading accounts you may have with a broker, including any online broker. These stocks are easy to value, as you can take the number of shares and multiply it by quote price. This category also includes stock you may have in a privately owned business. This may be a business you operate or one that is operated by another. Valuation of these types of businesses is more difficult in that there is no publicly traded market. In some cases, you can value them by determining the values of assets and subtracting the business debt. In some cases, it may be desirable to hire a business analyst to value the business. In any private corporation, you will need to have current balance sheets and lists of assets and liabilities.

14. *Interests in Partnerships or Joint Ventures:* If you have an interest in a partnership or are in business with another party, that information must be listed here. The same information that is required of a closely held business is required in this case.

15. *Bonds:* This includes public and private bonds. For public bonds, you will be able to obtain a current market quote—the same for bonds you have with a brokerage. Private bonds are more difficult, but you will still need to provide a value. In some cases, it may be possible to contact the entity that issued the bond to determine current value. The most common bonds individuals may have are savings bonds.

16. *Accounts Receivables:* You are required to provide a list of all who owe you money—their names and addresses and the amounts owed. In some cases, the value of the accounts receivable will be near the face value; in other cases, the value will be less, as the chance to collect on the account is riskier.

17. *Alimony, Maintenance, Support, and Property Settlements:* You will need to list any right you have to receive payments from a previous relationship. Most of these amounts will be protected.

You will also have to list any property you are still entitled to receive from a prior legal case, generally dissolution of marriage.

18. *Liquidated Debts, Including Tax Refunds:* The bankruptcy estate will have an interest in any tax refund you receive for the tax year in which you file, and for any tax refund you receive for a tax year prior to the bankruptcy filing that was not received prior to that date. The amount of the tax refund that is property of the bankruptcy estate will be a pro-rata share of the amount you will receive for the year.

19. *Equitable Future Interests:* You will need to disclose whether you are the beneficiary of a trust or other document that provides that you will receive property after another person dies. This is common in estate planning, where a parent or grandparent may want to live in a property, but may have transferred the remainder interest to family members.

20. *Interest in a Decedent's Estate, Death Benefit, Life Insurance Policy, or Trust:* If someone has passed away and you will receive anything, you must disclose this. This is also true if someone passes away within 180 days of your bankruptcy filing. The triggering event is the person's death, when you become entitled to receive the property—not when you actually receive the property.

21. *Contingent Claims:* These are claims you may have that have not been resolved, including claims for personal injury, worker's compensation, harassment, discrimination, or a disputed debt, or from termination, as well as many more.

22. *Patents, Copyrights, Intellectual Property:* If you have ever invented anything and obtained a patent, or written or published a book or article, list these assets here. If you have been receiving royalties, a value of your product will need to be obtained. This can be difficult, and you may need to consult an attorney.

23. *Licenses, Franchises, and Other Intangibles:* License in this sense means permission to do business or use a name or systems—for example, a license to run a liquor store, bar, or taxi service. The category also includes the right to use a particular name or business system to operate a business. A franchise is a

formal agreement providing you with the basis to conduct a particular business, such as a McDonald's or a Subway store, and generally, they describe an area where you will be the only person who can operate businesses under that name or system.

24. *Customer List:* If you have a business, you will have to provide a list of your customers. In some cases, this information may have value, but that depends on the extent of your list and the purpose.

25. *Cars, Trucks, Trailers, and Other Vehicles and Accessories:* You will have to list each vehicle you have and provide the bankruptcy trustee with copies of the titles. You will also have to provide a value for each, which can be obtained from the National Automobile Dealers Association (NADA) or Blue Book.

26. *Boats, Motors, and Accessories:* You will have to list each item and provide a value based on comparable sales.

27. *Aircraft and Accessories:* You will need to list each item, provide the trustee with the title, and obtain a value based on comparable sales.

28. *Office Equipment, Furnishings, and Supplies:* If you operate a business and have office equipment, furnishings, and supplies, you have to provide an account for the items. While you do not have to list every paper clip, you have to provide enough detail that the trustee can assess the value of the property. If you have any items that have a higher value, list them separately. Valuation should be based on comparable sales or replacement costs.

29. *Machinery, Fixtures:* These are generally more valuable items used in business. You should use replacement costs to value them.

30. *Inventory:* If you have a business and are selling items, you will need to provide a list of the items you have on hand. In valuing the asset, you should use liquidation costs.

31. *Animals:* All animals you have need to be listed. The trustee will not be interested in your pet unless that pet has a commercial value, such as for breeding. In general, the trustee is interested in livestock.

32. *Crops:* This is any farm product that may still be in the fields or in storage.

33. *Farm Equipment:* This is any machinery used in the operation of a farm, such as tractors, trailers, or plows.

34. *Farm Supplies, Chemicals, or Feed:* A list must be provided of any supplies, chemicals, or seeds, and a valuation should be based on replacement costs.

35. *Other Property:* If you have items you do not think fit any of the above categories, list them here.

In the bankruptcy, all your property and property interests will need to be listed. In addition, you will have to amend your property schedules after you file if within 180 days you become entitled to receive property from an inheritance, life insurance policy, or dissolution of marriage. In some cases, failure to list an asset may mean you will lose an asset that would otherwise be exempt.

Schedule C: Exempt Property

Exempt property is the single most important form in the bankruptcy. This is the list of property you say you are keeping. This benefit is available for individuals; corporations and partnerships are not able to claim exemptions. Exemptions are the acknowledgment that an individual needs something with which to start over.

The good news is that the information in Schedule B will duplicated for that property that is being claimed as exempt. In preparing the list of property, as in Schedule B, the property must be listed with enough detail to allow the trustee to be able to review the property, understand what the property is, determine whether the value is reasonable, and determine whether the property is such that the claimed exemption applies. The most difficult part of the form is the listing of the appropriate statute or law that exempts the property.

Where exemptions become far more complicated is in the choice of law that determines what property you may claim as exempt. Bankruptcy is a federal law, and as part the procedures, the relief you receive is determined by Congress, which has identified a list of property types that can be claimed as exempt. These types of property are referred to as the federal exemptions.

Preparing this schedule would simple if it ended there, but it does not. Each state has also identified a set of property that is exempt from collection. Congress also enacted a provision that allows the states to opt out of the federal exemptions. This means that in some states you have a choice to elect either the federal or the state exemptions. In other states, you must use the state exemptions. In any case, if a husband and wife file bankruptcy together, or one shortly after the other, they must both use the same set.

Whether you are able to claim the federal exemptions will depend on the state you live in. Currently, the following states allow the use of the federal exemptions: Arkansas, Connecticut, District of Columbia, Hawaii, Kentucky, Massachusetts, Minnesota, New Hampshire, New Jersey, New Mexico, Pennsylvania, Rhode Island, Texas, Vermont, Washington, and Wisconsin. In all other states, only state exemptions apply.

In addition to the list of property provided as exempt, the US Supreme Court has indicated certain assets are not the property of the bankruptcy estate, including ERISA-qualified retirement accounts.

The choice of exemptions will be determined by the state you live in. This is limited in cases where you have recently moved, as the Bankruptcy Code in part wants to prevent debtors from moving to states that have more lenient exemption schemes.

The federal exemptions will allow you to protect equity in your homestead, but limits that equity to $20,200 per person. Equity is determined by subtracting the amount of any liens from the value of the home. In addition, you will be able to protect equity in a motor vehicle, household goods and furnishings, jewelry, tools of your trade, accrued interest in a life insurance policy (cash value), alimony, and retirement accounts. All of the exemptions have a dollar limit.

In addition, the federal exemptions include what is called a "wild card exemption," which allows you to use up to one-half of the unused homestead exemption plus $1,075 on any property you select. In other words, you are able to protect property that would not otherwise be protected. This makes the federal exemptions attractive in many cases.

The state exemptions vary among states. Most debtors will have to use their state exemptions because the opt-out provision has been elected by the state. Even in cases where the debtor may choose to use the federal exemptions, state exemptions may be more attractive. For example, many states have a higher exemption limit for equity in a homestead. You will need to review your state's specific exemptions, but in general, you will be able to protect equity in a homestead, household goods and furnishings, and wearing apparel. The amount you can claim may vary wildly: Maryland, for instance, has an exemption for real or personal property of only $5,000, while the homestead exemption in Kansas has an unlimited value.

If property is not exempt, it will remain property of the bankruptcy estate. The Chapter 7 bankruptcy trustee will have to take possession of the asset and convert it to cash. In some cases, the trustee may be willing to sell the item back to you, but it is the trustee's job to obtain for the creditors as a whole the highest value for an item.

Schedule D: Secured Claims

This is a list of the creditors that have claims that are backed by collateral. Commonly these include real estate or car liens, though they may include personal property through a purchase money secured interest. A purchase money secured interest loan is common in the purchase of items such as jewelry or electronics. In general, a purchase money secured interest is obtained by a creditor by providing you credit to purchase a particular item. For example, if you were to purchase a computer and used a store credit card, they may be able to claim to have a purchase money secured interest in the computer. These types of secured loans are common with furniture and electronic stores. The key element is that the credit is being provided for the purchase of that item from a particular retailer.

A secured creditor has a claim that is protected by the value of the property on which it has a lien. You will have an option in the bankruptcy to surrender the property and discharge the debt, reaffirm the debt, or redeem the property. You may want to keep these debts, but you are still required to list all your assets and obligations. In addition, many mortgages and liens have language that requires that you provide notice of a bankruptcy filing.

Schedule E: Unsecured Priority Claims

Unsecured priority claims are debts that will generally not be discharged in the bankruptcy, even though they are not secured against property of the bankruptcy estate. They include debts such as child support, maintenance, alimony, taxes, extensions of credit in an involuntary cases, and deposits by individuals or wages that you owe another. Most of these interests are self-explanatory but there may be some confusion as to what is meant by deposits by individuals. These are claims by individuals for money that they have provided for the purchase, lease or rental of property, or for services for personal, family or household use that have not been provided.

Schedule F: Unsecured Claims

One of the most important forms in the bankruptcy, this schedule lists your unsecured creditors' claims—debts you anticipate will be discharged in your bankruptcy. This list will include accounts such as credit cards, medical bills, and personal loans. It will also include judgments that have been entered against you. Everybody you owe money to must be included in the list of creditors, even those you intend to pay after the bankruptcy. It is important that you provide accurate addresses so that the creditors may receive notice of the bankruptcy filing.

Schedule G: Executory Contracts and Unexpired Leases

An executory contract is one that has started but not finished—for example, an employment contract or an agreement to sell your home. An unexpired lease is one that has started but has not been completed for real estate, personal property, or a motor vehicle.

Schedule H: Co-Debtors

This means just what it says. You need to provide a list of any persons with whom you have co-signed a debt. For each, you will need to provide the name and address of the person and the amount of the debt in which they are listed as a co-debtor.

Schedule I: Income

It is important that you provide accurate information regarding your income, as it will be a basis for whether you qualify for Chapter 7 bankruptcy protection. The starting point is looking at your pay stubs and determining your monthly pay. If you are self-employed, you will need to look at your income and expense statements to determine what income you have. Income means funds you receive from any source regularly, including regular contributions from others. You will also need to provide information regarding payroll deductions taken for such items as taxes or health insurance.

Schedule J: Expenses

This schedule is important not only for the bankruptcy but for you to get a handle on your financial situation. Many people who file for bankruptcy protection do so because they do not have complete knowledge of their finances; in particular, they are not sure where their money is going. It is common for people to underestimate their expenses, particularly in food and clothing.

To complete the schedule, you will need to gather receipts and your checkbook. You should examine the numbers and make sure you are honest with them. I have found that people tend to under-report expenses such as food, as they will think they go to the grocery store twice a month and pay $150 each time, so they have a food expense of $300, forgetting that twice a week they pick up bread and milk. Expenses will include rent or home payments, vehicle payments, and maintenance, utilities, clothing, food, recreation, taxes, alimony, insurance, and maintenance-alimony or child support.

Declaration of Debtors Relating to Schedules

This is a simple but important form. By signing this form, you indicate to the US bankruptcy court that all of the information you have provided is true and correct, and you do so under the penalty of perjury.

Statement of Intention Regarding Secured Property

This form goes along with Schedule D: Secured Creditors. In the bankruptcy, you are required to indicate how you will deal with your secured creditors. Each of your secured creditors will be listed, along with the property that secures the lien. In each case, you will have to advise the court and the creditor of your intentions regarding the collateral. You will have three choices: reaffirm the debt, redeem the property, or surrender the property.

If you chose to reaffirm the debt, you agree to make the payments on the contract as if the bankruptcy never occurred. In other words, that debt will pass through. You will have the same obligations on the debt as you had prior to the bankruptcy, and the creditor will have the same rights. You will be able to maintain the property but will have to make the payments. If you fail to make a payment, that creditor will have the option of reposing/foreclosing the collateral. The creditor will also be able to maintain any state court action that it would have had, including the right to go after you for any deficiency between the value of the collateral and the amount of the debt.

Redemption requires that you pay the full value of the collateral, and the remaining debt will be discharged. The creditor is protected to the extent of the value of its security, but the remaining amount of the debt is discharged. You are required to provide full payment of the value of the item. For example, if you have a car worth $3,000, but you owe $8,000, you will be able to redeem the car by paying the creditor $3,000. Redemptions are rare in bankruptcy because you are required to pay the full amount of the value at one time and because it is often difficult for the debtor and the creditor to agree on a value.

Surrendering the property is just as it sounds. The secured creditor receives the property that is securing the loan. The creditor can sell the property or dispose of it any manner it wishes, but the debt will be discharged in the bankruptcy. The creditor receives the property but nothing else.

In addition, you will required to list the unexpired leases you may have. You have to advise the court and your creditors whether you wish to assume the lease or reject the lease. If you assume the lease, you are responsible as if the bankruptcy had not occurred, but you can keep the security. If you reject the lease, you are not obligated by its terms, but you must forfeit the property subject to the lease.

Statement of Financial Affairs

The Statement of Financial Affairs will provide the bankruptcy court and the Chapter 7 bankruptcy trustee a better idea of your overall true financial picture. The questions are meant to elicit information about transfers of property that a trustee can avoid as preferential or fraudulent. As with all of your schedules, you sign the Statement of Financial Affairs under oath. Following are the questions you will have to answer:

1. *Income from Employment or Operation of Business:* You will need to list the income you have received from an employer or in your business for the current year, as well as the previous two years.
2. *Income Other Than from Employment or Operation of Business:* You will need to list any income you received from any other source for the current year and the two years prior. This may

include income from sources such as cashing in a retirement account or the sale of stock.

3. *Payments to Creditors:* The trustee will want to see whom you have paid and whether any of those payments may have been by preference. The trustee is looking for payments above a normal payment made to a creditor so that the creditor received more than it would have in a Chapter 7 bankruptcy. The trustee can review these transactions for most creditors for the previous ninety days and can go back an entire year for friends, family members, and insiders. The trustee can sue the individuals who were paid and require that they return the funds to the bankruptcy estate to be distributed.

4. *Suits, Administrative Proceedings, Executions, Garnishments, and Attachments:* You will have to list any lawsuit to which you are a party and disclose whether you have lost any property through creditor actions, such as a garnishment or attachment. Any property that was taken by a creditor in the ninety days prior to the bankruptcy filing may be recoverable by the bankruptcy trustee and in some cases by you.

5. *Repossession or Foreclosures:* You will have to list any property you lost, the name of the creditor, and the date.

6. *Assignments and Receiverships:* You will have to provide information regarding any property you may have assigned to another party and any receivership to which you may be a party.

7. *Gifts:* You will need to provide a list of any gifts you gave to any family member with a value of $200 or more in the past year. If you gave any other gifts, you will have to list them if they had a value of over $100.

8. *Losses:* You will need to provide a list of any losses you suffered in the last year, including property losses due to a fire, a storm, or gambling. You will also have to provide information on whether the loss was covered by insurance.

9. *Payments on Debt Counseling or Bankruptcy:* If you have obtained the services of an attorney or bankruptcy petition preparer, you will have to list the amounts you paid to them.

10. *Other Transfers:* This is a catchall provision. If you had property in the last year and you no longer have it, and you do not know where to list that transfer, you need to list it here.

11. *Closed Accounts:* If you have had a bank account or a brokerage account at any time and have closed it, you will need to list it here and provide the date of closing and the balance on the date of closing.

12. *Safe Deposit Boxes:* If you have a safe deposit box with any institution, you will need to provide the name and address of the institution, the names of all persons with access to the box, and a list of property in the box.

13. *Setoffs:* If you owe money to someone who owed you money, and the person set off the amount you owed against the amount he or she owed, it needs to be listed here.

14. *Property Held for Another Person:* Do you have property in your possession that is not your property? You need to list that property here. You must include a description of the property and for whom you are holding it.

15. *Prior Addresses:* If you have moved, you will need to list the address of any prior residence, the name you used when living there, and the dates of occupancy. This will require you to provide any address that you have had in the past three years.

The above questions will need to be completed in all cases. An additional set of information will be applicable only in limited cases, mostly where a business is involved:

16. *Spouses and Former Spouses:* In community property states, you will be required to list any spouse you have been to whom you have been married in the past eight years.

17. *Environmental Information:* If you have a property that has any environmental issues, you will have to provide that information here.

18. *Business Information:* If you have a business, you will need to provide information on it, including the name and address of the business, the tax identification number, location of books and records, and the type and purpose of the business.

19. *Books and Records:* You will need to provide a location of all books and records and the names and addresses of any bookkeepers or accountants for the two years prior to filing.

20. *Inventories:* You will have to list the date of any inventory and the person who conducted the inventory, as well the value of the assets.

21. *Partners, Officers, Directors, and Shareholders:* For any business, you will need to provide the list of any individuals that meet this description.

22. *Former Partners, Officers, Directors, or Shareholders:* If someone left the business in the past year, you will need to provide his or her name, address, and date of withdrawal.

23. *Withdrawals from a Business:* If any person or entity took money from the business, you will need to provide the name and address of the recipient, as well as the date he or she received the payment.

24. *Tax Consolidation Group:* This provision will not apply in an individual case. It only applies in cases where there is a corporation where there may be several layers, such as a parent corporation and subsidiary.

25. *Pension Funds.* This provision will not apply for an individual but is a requirement for a corporation. It requires corporations to list the name and federal tax identification number of any retirement plan that debtor as an employee has been required to contribute to in the past six years.

Means Test

The statement of current income and means test calculation is one of the most important forms in the bankruptcy. It serves two related functions—first, to determine whether you are exempt from the means test, and second, if you are not exempt, to determine whether a presumption of abuse is present. The first function will compare your income based on a family of your size in your district. The district is the geographic area in which you live. If your income is below the median income, you will be able to file for Chapter 7 bankruptcy protection without any further calculations. The means test is also not required for a disabled veteran whose indebtedness occurred during a time when he or she was on active duty.

If your income is higher than the median income, the means test is prepared, determining from your income and expenses whether there is a presumption of abuse if you continue with the filing. If you are unmarried or married and living apart or legally separated from your spouse, then only your income needs to be included, but if you are married and filing jointly or living together, both incomes will need to be included.

The income to be listed is the average monthly income from all sources for the past six months. The form lists various forms of income and has a catchall section for any income that may not otherwise be included. Income will also include amounts you receive regularly from friends or family members.

Once we have determined your income, the next step is to determine the deductions. For the purposes of means testing, there are two types of deductions—those allowed by the Internal Revenue Service (IRS) and actual expenses. The IRS has both national and local standards for living and transportation expenses. The IRS deductions are standard deductions and are not related to the actual expense. They are determined by the place of residence, income, and family size. The means test will also ask you for the actual amount of the mortgage payments you have to make over the next sixty months. The total of the permitted monthly expenses will be listed and then taken from your income to determine disposable income.

The basic rule is that a presumption of abuse will arise if your monthly disposable income multiplied by sixty is equal to or greater than $10,950, or 25 percent of your unsecured debt.

Notice to Individual Consumer Debtor under Section 342(b) of the Bankruptcy Code

In every bankruptcy case, you will be required to review a statement that briefly describes the services of credit counseling agencies and the purposes, benefits, and costs of the various chapters of the bankruptcy, and informs you regarding bankruptcy crimes. This form provides information to you and serves as a warning that if you are dishonest, the information you have provided or failed to provide may lead to criminal prosecution. It also lets you know that the information you have provided may be shared with law enforcement authorities. You need to be sure you fully, and honestly, answer the questions asked in the bankruptcy petition and schedules, as the information is being provided under oath.

Now that you have completed the bankruptcy petition and schedules, reviewed them, and signed them, you will be able to file them with the bankruptcy court. You will also have to file the Certificate of Credit Counseling and pay the $299 filing fee. The court will then send out notices advising the creditors of the bankruptcy filing, listing the trustee, and setting a date for the meeting of creditors. The filing of the bankruptcy petition and schedules begins the bankruptcy.

10

What Is an Automatic Stay?

When you file your bankruptcy petition and schedules, you will immediately be protected from actions by your creditors that are an attempt to collect on the debt. The relief comes from the filing of the bankruptcy—not when the creditors actually receive notice. (11 USC 362(a)) The stay prevents:

- The commencement or continuation of any judicial proceeding to collect on a debt
- The enforcement of a judgment
- Any act to obtain possession of property from the bankruptcy estate
- Any action to create, perfect, or enforce against property of the bankruptcy estate any lien
- Any act to collect a claim
- The set-off of any claim that arose in connection with a debt that was incurred prior to the bankruptcy filing

The stay does not prevent certain acts and proceedings from continuing, including:

- Criminal proceedings against the debtor
- Commencement or continuation of an action to establish paternity or to establish or modify domestic support obligations
- Collection of domestic support obligations from non-estate property

- The withholding of income for a domestic support obligation
- The withholding or suspension of a driver's license or professional license
- The reporting of overdue child support
- The interception of a tax refund
- The enforcement of police powers
- An action of a landlord of non-residential real property to gain possession of the real property

The automatic stay remains in effect, unless the court terminates it earlier, as long as property stays in the bankruptcy estate, until the court grants a discharge, or until the case is closed, whichever occurs first.

A creditor may seek relief of the automatic stay in a bankruptcy. This is a request for the court to allow the creditor to proceed with a collection effort against a specific piece of property. This frequently occurs when a creditor is secured by property and you have failed to pay. The court will grant the relief if it believes the property will not be property of the bankruptcy estate and it is not necessary for an effective reorganization. As bankruptcy is liquidation and not repayment, this is almost always the case.

11

What Is the Meeting of the Creditors?

The meeting of creditors will be set not less than twenty nor more than forty days after the filing of the voluntary Chapter 7 bankruptcy case. It will be held in a location designated by the US Trustee. The notice that is sent to creditors advising them of the bankruptcy filing will also advise them of the meeting of creditors.

Any creditor may appear at the meeting to ask questions of you, but in practice, most creditors will not make an appearance. At the meeting, the bankruptcy trustee will place you under oath. The trustee will verify your identity by a picture ID and proof of your Social Security number. The trustee will ask you for your name and address. Frequently they will ask for a telephone number. They will inquire as to whether the information in the petition and schedules is true and accurate.

When you attend the meeting of creditors, you will have to bring documents so that the trustee can verify the information in the bankruptcy petition and schedules. This documentation will include not only the picture ID and Social Security number information, but also copies of bank account statements, pay stubs, vehicle titles, and credit card statements. The trustee will look for verification of the information contained in the schedules and will try to see whether he or she will be able to bring any property into the bankruptcy estate.

12

Corporations under Chapter 7

Corporations, partnerships, limited liability companies, and limited liability partnerships are all eligible to file for protection under 11 USC Chapter 7 (Chapter 7 of the Bankruptcy Code). The bankruptcy will be similar to, but not exactly like, a personal filing.

The petition will be the same; the name of the corporation will be listed as the name; and the corporation's address will be the address. As this case is a corporate case, you will not be an individual signatory, but rather you would file on behalf of the corporation, under the penalty of perjury, that the information is correct and that you have the authority to sign. In some cases, if you are a railroad, stockbroker, commodities broker, or single asset real estate corporation, there will be additional requirements, and you should consult with an attorney. If the corporation has many assets, you may also want to consult with an attorney.

The schedules for the corporation are similar, with the exception that there is no Schedule C-Exempt Property. A corporation under Chapter 7 is liquidated. This means that it is not able to exempt any property; rather, all of its assets are converted to cash, and the funds are distributed to the creditors.

In some cases, the bankruptcy trustee may believe the corporation has more value as an ongoing entity and may attempt to operate the business in an effort to sell it, but this is difficult and time-consuming and generally involves an influx of capital from a lender that is not often available. In many cases, when small corporations are liquidated, they have no value to the unsecured creditors, as all of the assets were secured.

The Statement of Financial Affairs will be the same as in an individual case, but requires additional detail. The bankruptcy trustee will still look for preferential payments to creditors and insiders, as well as fraudulent transfers, but he or she will pay particular attention to payments made to officers and shareholders.

In a corporate filing, all the information required for corporations will need to be completed and the information provided to the trustee, including the information in questions 17 to 25 on environmental concerns; the nature of the business; the books and records; who worked on the books; when inventories were completed and by whom; a list of current partners, officers, directors, and shareholders; a list of former partners, officers, directors, and shareholders; withdrawals from the partnership or distributions by corporations; and pension fund information. In the case of a corporation, the trustee will review this information in detail to ensure that everything was done above board.

In a corporate bankruptcy, fewer documents must be filed than in the case of an individual. There is no requirement that the corporation take either the pre-filing or the post-filing education class. There is no requirement that the corporation file Schedule C-Exempt Property, as a corporation is not able to claim any exemptions. A corporation is not required to file a Statement of Intention (the document that indicates whether you will reaffirm, redeem, or surrender secured property), as any secured property will be surrendered, so the form is not necessary. There will be no property from which payments could be made. There is no requirement to file the Notice to Consumer Debtors, as this is not a consumer case. There is also no requirement to file the Means Test Calculation.

After the submission of the bankruptcy petition and schedules, the bankruptcy trustee will be appointed. The meeting of creditors will be scheduled, and the trustee will be able to ask the party who signed the bankruptcy petition and schedules questions to verify the information contained in the schedules. The trustee will have the same rights and duties to convert the non-exempt assets to the bankruptcy case. The trustee will also be able to avoid preferential and fraudulent transfers in an effort to maximize the bankruptcy estate. The trustee will then distribute the funds to the unsecured creditors. This will effectively end the business.

One thing that you need to be aware of is that the corporation filing bankruptcy will not affect any of your personal obligations. The bankruptcy will be able to discharge only the obligations of the corporation. It is not uncommon in small businesses that the corporation may have debt that is secured by a personal guaranty of one or more of the officers or shareholders. This is common with banks and credit cards. These personal guaranties are not affected by the bankruptcy filing and will remain the obligation of those filing.

13

Discharge Basics

A discharge in bankruptcy releases the debtor from personal liability on a debt. In other words, the debtor no longer has any legal responsibility to pay the debt, and the creditor may not collect on that debt. The discharge is a permanent order prohibiting creditors from taking action to collect on these debts. This prohibition includes legal actions, phone calls, and other communications with a debtor. With secured liens, the order prevents the creditor from collecting on a debt, but not enforcing the lien; that is, the lien holder is able to repossess the collateral, but cannot go after a deficiency. Many, but not all, debts may be discharged in a bankruptcy.

The timing of a discharge will vary, depending on the chapter of the Bankruptcy Code under which the petition is filed. In a Chapter 7 bankruptcy, the court usually grants the discharge when the time has expired for a creditor to file an objection to the discharge of its debt. This is generally sixty days after the date first set for the meeting of creditors. This is generally three to four months after the bankruptcy petition has been filed with the US bankruptcy court.

In cases under Chapters 11, 12, and 13, the court generally grants the discharge as soon as possible after the debtor completes the payments called for in the plan. This means that the discharge may not occur for three to five years after the initial filing of the bankruptcy petition.

One of the bankruptcy reforms that were passed in 2005 was an education requirement. This includes a requirement that the debtor take a class to file a consumer bankruptcy under Chapters 7 and 13. It also requires that debtors take a second class prior to receiving a discharge. If proof of completion of this second class is not filed with the bankruptcy court, the court may deny the debtor a discharge. The second class is meant to address issues regarding financial management. The Bankruptcy Code has only limited exceptions to this requirement, such as the failure of a class to be available in a district, that the debtor is in the military, or that the debtor is incapacitated or disabled.

The discharge of debts is generally an automatic process. The notice will be sent to all the creditors, and the debtor will automatically receive a discharge. This does not include creditors who file an objection to discharge with the bankruptcy court prior to the date that the discharge is granted. This date will be provided on the Notice of Commencement of Case sent by the United States Bankruptcy Court and is usually sixty days after the date of the meeting of creditors. The notice that is sent to the creditors is not specific. It is a notice that generally states that the debts have been discharged, and attempts to collect on the debt may be a violation of the discharge order. It also advises that attempts to collect on those debts may subject those creditors to punishment for contempt.

Not all debts are discharged. The actual debts that are discharged will vary somewhat among the chapters of the Bankruptcy Code. The Bankruptcy Code prevents certain debts from being discharged. 11 USC 523 (a). This means that these debts will still have to be repaid after the bankruptcy has been completed.

There are various reasons that Congress has granted special treatment of these debts. Some of the exemptions are for policy reasons, and some are to prevent the ability of debtor to be excused from improper behavior. In most cases, the exception to discharge is automatic, meaning that the creditor does not have to take any action to protect its right to collect on the debt. In some cases, the creditor is required to object to the discharge, and the bankruptcy court must determine whether the debt meets the exception to discharge.

The most common types of debts that will not be discharged are certain types of tax debts; spousal or child support, maintenance, or alimony; marital obligations; debts for willful and malicious injuries to persons or property; debts for personal injury caused by the debtor's intoxicated driving; and debts owed to certain retirement plans. Though most education (student) loans are also exempted from discharge, the debtor may seek to have them discharged for undue hardship, but this is relief that many districts rarely grant. If a debt was incurred by fraud or the malicious conduct of the debtor, it may be exempted from discharge, but only after the creditor brings an action, similar to a lawsuit, and the bankruptcy court finds a reason for the exemption from discharge. In those cases, if the creditor fails to object, the debt is discharged.

Chapter 13 provides for a slightly broader discharge of debts. In a Chapter 13 bankruptcy, debts for willful and malicious damages to property, debts incurred to pay non-dischargeable taxes, and debts arising from a property settlement in a dissolution of marriage proceeding would be discharged. The discharge, however, is not granted until all the required payments are made.

The debtor may seek a hardship discharge in some limited circumstances. This is a request for discharge relief even though the debtor has not completed all required payments. These hardship discharges are available to debtors who failed to make payments required by the plan only because of circumstances beyond the debtor's control. A hardship discharge is also available under Chapter 12, but the standard is slightly different. In those cases, the court views the request and determines whether there are circumstances for which the debtor should not justly be held accountable. This is a lower standard of proof.

A debtor in a Chapter 7 bankruptcy does not have an absolute right to a discharge. It is possible for a party in interest to file an objection to the debtor receiving a discharge. This party may be a creditor, the bankruptcy trustee, or the US trustee.

The notice sent to the creditors in the beginning of a case will set the deadlines for creditors to take action. The creditor must file an action with the bankruptcy court prior to the bar date set in that notice. This does not mean that the issue must be decided before that date, only that the action must be filed with the court. This is a type of lawsuit referred to as an adversary proceeding.

The court may deny a Chapter 7 discharge for a number of reasons. These are listed in 11 USC 727 (a) of the Bankruptcy Code and include failing to provide the required tax forms and failure to complete the second course on personal financial management. They also include actions that may be seen as the debtor being dishonest, such as transferring property or concealing property with the intent to defraud creditors, destruction or concealment of records, perjury, fraudulent conduct, failure to account for loss of assets, violation of a court order, or filing the bankruptcy within the time frames that bar the discharge. These actions are based on the misconduct of the debtor. The party requesting that the discharge be denied will be required to prove all of the elements of these exceptions.

In Chapter 12 and Chapter 13 cases, discharge is generally granted upon the completion of the payments under the plan. This will not happen if the debtor fails to complete the course on personal financial management or receives a discharge in a previous bankruptcy within the applicable period. Creditors do not have a right to object to a discharge; instead, they have a right to object to the plan.

It is possible for a debtor to receive a second discharge in a later bankruptcy case, but at least eight years must pass since they received a discharge under Chapter 7 or Chapter 11. If the debtor received a bankruptcy discharge under Chapter 12 or 13, the debtor must wait at least six years, unless the debtor paid all unallowed unsecured claims in the earlier case or repaid at least 70 percent of the allowed unsecured claims, and the plan was made in good faith, and the payments represented the debtors' best efforts. A debtor is ineligible for a Chapter 13 discharge if he or she received a discharge under a Chapter 7, 11, or 12 case filed four years before the current case. The limit is two years for a Chapter 13 discharge.

In cases where a discharge was granted, it may be revoked under certain circumstances, including cases where the debtor obtained the discharge under fraudulent circumstances. It can also occur in cases where the debtor became entitled to receive property after the bankruptcy filing that was property of the bankruptcy estate and failed to disclose this to the bankruptcy trustee. A discharge may also be revoked in those cases where the debtor failed to obey a court order or under some circumstances for failing to respond to a material question.

Creditors are barred from collecting debts that have been discharged. If a creditor attempts to collect a discharged debt, the debtor can file a motion with the bankruptcy court, reopening the case and requesting that the court address the matter. The court then reviews the matter and can sanction the creditor for violating the discharge injunction.

14

Alternatives to Bankruptcy

There are several alternatives to bankruptcy, including out-of-court settlements with creditors. This may be accomplished on a case-by-case basis where the debtor negotiates with a creditor for a reduction in the amount owed or the amount of the payments. The debtor may do this either by himself or herself, hire an attorney, or contact a debt counseling agency. This may be done in a number of different manners, including:

Offers in Compromise

An offer in compromise is a negotiated settlement in which the debtor and the creditor negotiate a payment to settle an account in full. The amount that will be received is generally a percentage of the amount that is due. These generally require a lump sum payment. Many agencies will act on behalf of debtors by setting up a payment plan, whereby the debtor will make a monthly payment to an agency, which will hold onto the funds and then negotiate a creditor-by-creditor settlement. Debtors need to be aware that there may be negative tax consequences, as the IRS may view the amount that was discharged as income.

Debt Consolidation Plan

Often creditors will work with an agency that will set up a monthly payment and forward those funds to the creditors. This is similar to a Chapter 13 bankruptcy, but as there is no court action, there is no requirement that a creditor agree to a proposed payment plan.

Restructuring Secured Loan

Many debtors will seek to take out loans against the equity in their homes. This must be done with caution. The debtor needs to be sure that he or she will be able to make the new payments or risk losing the home.

15

Frequently Asked Questions

What is bankruptcy?

Bankruptcy is a legal process that allows debtors who are in over their heads with debt a chance for a fresh start. They can be individuals, couples, or corporations. There are various chapters of the Bankruptcy Code, each offering different types of relief, from a fresh start under Chapter 7 to reorganization under Chapter 13.

How do I know whether I should file bankruptcy?

Bankruptcy, for most people, is voluntary. It is a request from the court to grant a discharge (release) from your debt. It is an option for a person or couple that cannot pay their debt and are falling further and further behind. There is no simple test, but what you should consider is the amount of debt you have, the assets you have, whether you will be able to discharge your debt, whether you will be able to keep your assets, and the impact the bankruptcy will have on your credit. If you have unsecured debt that cannot be repaid in five to ten years, bankruptcy may be an option.

How will bankruptcy affect my credit?

Bankruptcy is a negative factor on your credit. It will lower your credit score, and creditors will consider the fact that you filed in determining whether they will loan you money. The bankruptcy, however, may provide you with a place to start the rebuilding process. The elimination of the debts, combined with positive credit actions, such as paying on a mortgage or rent, will slowly let you rebuild your credit.

Will I ever be able to get a loan?

Yes. It may take time, but slowly your ability to get a loan will return.

I have a small business that is incorporated. Can I file for bankruptcy?

Yes, a small business can file for bankruptcy protection. In many cases, the filing may be a Chapter 7 (liquidation), which will wind up the corporation, sell the assets, and use those funds to pay the creditors.

What is Chapter 7?

Chapter 7 refers to Chapter 7 of the Bankruptcy Code. It is referred to as a fresh start. A Chapter 7 bankruptcy does not involve a repayment plan; rather, any non-exempt property will be sold off by the bankruptcy trustee, and those funds will be distributed to the creditors in proportion to the amount they are owed. A debtor is able to obtain a discharge from the remainder of the debt.

Should I file for bankruptcy under Chapter 7?

Chapter 7 bankruptcy is effective for individuals who have unsecured debt that is dischargeable in a bankruptcy, who have few assets that are non-exempt, and whose income is below the median income for a family of their size in their state.

What happens when I file for Chapter 7 bankruptcy protection?

The debtor prepares a bankruptcy petition and schedules that are filed with the court. This petition and schedules will include a list of assets and a list of exempt property. The bankruptcy trustee will review the petition and schedules and administer the bankruptcy estate. This will include the collection and sale of the non-exempt property of the bankruptcy estate. The proceeds of those sales will then be distributed to the creditors.

What is Chapter 13?

Chapter 13 refers to Chapter 13 of the Bankruptcy Code. A Chapter 13 bankruptcy involves a repayment plan that can take up to sixty months. The debtor makes payments to the Chapter 13 trustee, who then makes payments to the creditors. The payment plan is approved by the bankruptcy judge and may be a percentage of the amount that is owed.

Should I file for bankruptcy under Chapter 13?

A Chapter 13 bankruptcy is appropriate for a person who has an income that is higher than the median income or who has debts that will not be discharged in a Chapter 7 bankruptcy. Some of these debts include many taxes or fines. In addition, a Chapter 13 bankruptcy is appropriate for an individual who is filing a bankruptcy to prevent the foreclosure of a home. The provisions of Chapter 13 allow for a stay of the foreclosure and the option of repaying the mortgage arrearages on a payment plan.

What is Chapter 12?

Chapter 12 refers to Chapter 12 of the Bankruptcy Code. In some respects, it is similar to Chapter 13, as it has a payment plan, but the code provides for specifics that are meant to benefit family farmers.

What is Chapter 11?

Chapter 11 refers to Chapter 11 of the Bankruptcy Code. When you are watching the news, and the finance reporter talks of a corporate bankruptcy, it is most likely under this chapter. The provisions of Chapter 11 allow for the reorganization of a corporate entity or an individual. One of the key elements in a bankruptcy is that the corporation must shift its focus from its shareholders to its creditors.

Are there other chapters of the Bankruptcy Code?

In addition to Chapters 7, 11, 12, and 13, the Bankruptcy Code contains Chapter 9, which is for municipalities, and Chapter 15, which is for international bankruptcies.

How often can I file for bankruptcy protection?

A person can file for Chapter 7 bankruptcy protection eight years after previously filing. A Chapter 13 bankruptcy can be filed even more often.

What does it cost to file bankruptcy?

In any bankruptcy, you will be required to pay a filing fee of between $274 and $299. In addition, each individual must take a class before filing bankruptcy and a class after filing bankruptcy and before a discharge. The costs of these classes range from $10 to $75 each. Many people will also have the costs of an attorney, which will vary from district to district.

Do I need an attorney?

There is no requirement that an individual be represented by an attorney to file bankruptcy, but bankruptcy is a statutorily created process that has specific requirements that, if not followed, may cause concern or lead to the loss of property that would otherwise be exempt.

What property can I keep after a bankruptcy?

Every state is different in the specific property that you can keep, but in general, you will be able to protect your home, a vehicle, retirement accounts, and your household goods and furnishings.

Can I keep my house and/or car after I file for bankruptcy?

The answer to this question is yes in most cases. In a bankruptcy, you will be able to keep the house or vehicle if you reaffirm the debt that is secured by the property and you are able to protect the equity with an exemption.

Will a bankruptcy eliminate all debts?

A bankruptcy will not eliminate certain debts, such as debts for marital obligations, child support, alimony, debts incurred by a DWI conviction, and criminal fines. Many taxes cannot be discharged. In many cases, secured debts will not be discharged.

Can I erase my student loans in a bankruptcy?

For the most part, student loans will not be discharged by a bankruptcy. For a student loan to be discharged, a legal action must be commenced, and the court must find that paying the loans would cause an undue hardship.

Can I file on a debt that has gone to judgment?

The simple answer is yes. The fact that a creditor has received a judgment does not exclude the debt from being dischargeable.

Will I have to go to court?

In most cases, the answer is no. You will have to go to a Section 341 meeting (meeting of creditors), where the bankruptcy trustee will verify your identity and ask you questions about your bankruptcy petition and schedules.

What will happen to my credit?

The best answer is that it will depend on how bad your credit is when you file. In any case, the bankruptcy is a detrimental to your credit, but it may allow you a way to start to rebuild.

Will I be able to get a credit card?

It most cases you will be able to get a credit card.

Will my utility service be affected?

If you owe money to a utility, and they suffer a loss, they will be able to require that you pay a security deposit, but they will be required to provide you service.

Will I be discriminated against for filing bankruptcy?

Federal law prevents discrimination against bankruptcy debtors by governmental units with respect to employment or the granting of licenses, permits, franchises, or similar grants; by private employers with respect to employment; and in the issuance of student loans.

What is the effect of a bankruptcy on co-signors?

The bankruptcy will have no effect on co-signors; they will still be obligated to pay the debt.

Does my spouse have to file bankruptcy if I do?

The simple answer is no. There is no requirement that both spouses file bankruptcy. In many cases, it makes sense for both to file, particularly if they have much common debt, as the non-filing spouse will still be obligated on those accounts.

If I file bankruptcy, will it stop the collection calls?

Once a bankruptcy has been filed, there is a provision called the automatic stay that indicates that all collection efforts must cease.

How long after filing will the creditors stop calling?

The provisions of the automatic stay take effect upon the filing of the bankruptcy petition and schedules with the court. The notices are generally sent out five to ten days after the filing date. The creditors will stop collection efforts once they have received notice.

What is a discharge in bankruptcy?

A discharge is the court order that prevents creditors from collecting on their debts. This is the relief the debtor seeks.

When do I receive my discharge?

A discharge is granted against those creditors that have not objected to the discharge of their debt sixty days after the date of the Section 341 hearing (meeting of creditors).

What happens when a creditor objects to a discharge?

There is the commencement of a lawsuit in the bankruptcy court, where the bankruptcy judge will have to determine whether the debt may be discharged in the bankruptcy.

What types of debts will not be discharged?

As previously discussed, the bankruptcy will not discharge debts for marital obligations, child support, maintenance or alimony, student loans, debts incurred by a DWI, and many tax debts. In addition, debts incurred by fraud or with the intent of including them in the bankruptcy will not be discharged.

Can the discharge be revoked?

The court can revoke a discharge—for example, if a debtor does not cooperate with the bankruptcy trustee or does not complete the duties that are required.

What are my duties if I file bankruptcy?

You will be required to file a bankruptcy petition and schedules with accurate information. You are also required to cooperate with the trustee in turning over the property of the bankruptcy estate and providing information for the trustee to verify the information you provided.

What happens if I fail to list a creditor in my bankruptcy?

In most cases, the debt will not be discharged. In some cases, such as a no-asset bankruptcy case, the debt will still be discharged upon notice to the creditor. This is allowed in those cases because the creditor was not harmed by the failure to be listed.

After I receive my discharge, can I still pay some of my debts?

Yes, if you have received a discharge, this will prevent creditors from being able to collect from you, but you can voluntarily repay a debt. This may happen because a debt is owed to a family member or credit with that creditor, such as a doctor, is important.

What is means testing?

Means testing is a method of determining a person's eligibility to file for Chapter 7 bankruptcy protection. The first calculation under the means test is whether your income is higher or lower than the median income for a family of your size in your district. If your income is lower than this amount, you are exempt from the means test. If your income is higher, a calculation is made using IRS deductions and some of your income to determine whether you have the ability to fund a repayment plan.

Glossary of Bankruptcy Terms

Automatic stay: The bankruptcy provision that provides that creditors cannot take any action to collect on their debt during the bankruptcy.

Bankruptcy estate: All the property a debtor has or has an interest in on the date of the bankruptcy filing.

Bankruptcy trustee: A person appointed by the court, in most cases, who administers the bankruptcy estate, liquidating the non-exempt property in a Chapter 7 bankruptcy, accepting payments in a Chapter 13, and then distributing the funds to the creditors.

Chapter 7: A bankruptcy filed under Chapter 7 of the Bankruptcy Code; often referred to as a fresh start or liquidation. The bankruptcy estate is liquidated, and the money is split among the creditors as a whole.

Chapter 13: A bankruptcy filed under Chapter 13 of the Bankruptcy Code. A repayment plan is developed in which the debtor makes payments to the bankruptcy trustee, who disburses those payments to creditors.

Creditor: A person or entity to whom a debt is owed.

Debtor: A person who owes another person or entity a debt.

Discharge: The relief sought in a bankruptcy. It is specifically an order of the US bankruptcy court that states that a creditor who received notice of a bankruptcy filing in time to submit a claim or object to the discharge of debt may not take any action to collect on that debt.

Means test: A test implemented by Congress as part of the bankruptcy reform of 2005 in an effort to force more debtors into Chapter 13 repayment plans. It compares the income for a family against the median income for a family of similar size. The assumption is that if the family's income is higher than this amount, a Chapter 13 Bankruptcy is appropriate.

Reaffirmation agreement: An agreement between the debtor and a creditor in which the debtor agrees to continue to make payments to the creditor after the bankruptcy has been discharged.

Secured debt: Money owed to a creditor that has a lien on property, such as a home or a vehicle.

Unsecured debt: Debt owed to a creditor that does not have an interest in property.

Appendices

APPENDIX A

B1-VOLUNTARY PETITION

B1 (Official Form 1) (4/10)

UNITED STATES BANKRUPTCY COURT	VOLUNTARY PETITION
Name of Debtor (if individual, enter Last, First, Middle):	Name of Joint Debtor (Spouse) (Last, First, Middle):
All Other Names used by the Debtor in the last 8 years (include married, maiden, and trade names):	All Other Names used by the Joint Debtor in the last 8 years (include married, maiden, and trade names):
Last four digits of Soc. Sec. or Individual-Taxpayer I.D. (ITIN)/Complete EIN (if more than one, state all):	Last four digits of Soc. Sec. or Individual-Taxpayer I.D. (ITIN)/Complete EIN (if more than one, state all):
Street Address of Debtor (No. and Street, City, and State): ZIP CODE	Street Address of Joint Debtor (No. and Street, City, and State): ZIP CODE
County of Residence or of the Principal Place of Business:	County of Residence or of the Principal Place of Business:
Mailing Address of Debtor (if different from street address): ZIP CODE	Mailing Address of Joint Debtor (if different from street address): ZIP CODE
Location of Principal Assets of Business Debtor (if different from street address above): ZIP CODE	

Type of Debtor (Form of Organization) (Check one box.)	Nature of Business (Check one box.)	Chapter of Bankruptcy Code Under Which the Petition is Filed (Check one box.)
☐ Individual (includes Joint Debtors) See Exhibit D on page 2 of this form. ☐ Corporation (includes LLC and LLP) ☐ Partnership ☐ Other (If debtor is not one of the above entities, check this box and state type of entity below.)	☐ Health Care Business ☐ Single Asset Real Estate as defined in 11 U.S.C. § 101(51B) ☐ Railroad ☐ Stockbroker ☐ Commodity Broker ☐ Clearing Bank ☐ Other	☐ Chapter 7 ☐ Chapter 15 Petition for ☐ Chapter 9 Recognition of a Foreign ☐ Chapter 11 Main Proceeding ☐ Chapter 12 ☐ Chapter 15 Petition for ☐ Chapter 13 Recognition of a Foreign Nonmain Proceeding
	Tax-Exempt Entity (Check box, if applicable.) ☐ Debtor is a tax-exempt organization under Title 26 of the United States Code (the Internal Revenue Code).	Nature of Debts (Check one box.) ☐ Debts are primarily consumer ☐ Debts are primarily debts, defined in 11 U.S.C. business debts. § 101(8) as "incurred by an individual primarily for a personal, family, or house- hold purpose."

Filing Fee (Check one box.)	Chapter 11 Debtors
☐ Full Filing Fee attached. ☐ Filing Fee to be paid in installments (applicable to individuals only). Must attach signed application for the court's consideration certifying that the debtor is unable to pay fee except in installments. Rule 1006(b). See Official Form 3A. ☐ Filing Fee waiver requested (applicable to chapter 7 individuals only). Must attach signed application for the court's consideration. See Official Form 3B.	Check one box: ☐ Debtor is a small business debtor as defined in 11 U.S.C. § 101(51D). ☐ Debtor is not a small business debtor as defined in 11 U.S.C. § 101(51D). Check if: ☐ Debtor's aggregate noncontingent liquidated debts (excluding debts owed to insiders or affiliates) are less than $2,343,300 (amount subject to adjustment on 4/01/13 and every three years thereafter). - Check all applicable boxes: ☐ A plan is being filed with this petition. ☐ Acceptances of the plan were solicited prepetition from one or more classes of creditors, in accordance with 11 U.S.C. § 1126(b).

Statistical/Administrative Information		THIS SPACE IS FOR COURT USE ONLY
☐ Debtor estimates that funds will be available for distribution to unsecured creditors. ☐ Debtor estimates that, after any exempt property is excluded and administrative expenses paid, there will be no funds available for distribution to unsecured creditors.		

Estimated Number of Creditors

☐ 1-49	☐ 50-99	☐ 100-199	☐ 200-999	☐ 1,000-5,000	☐ 5,001-10,000	☐ 10,001-25,000	☐ 25,001-50,000	☐ 50,001-100,000	☐ Over 100,000

Estimated Assets

☐ $0 to $50,000	☐ $50,001 to $100,000	☐ $100,001 to $500,000	☐ $500,001 to $1 million	☐ $1,000,001 to $10 million	☐ $10,000,001 to $50 million	☐ $50,000,001 to $100 million	☐ $100,000,001 to $500 million	☐ $500,000,001 to $1 billion	☐ More than $1 billion

Estimated Liabilities

☐ $0 to $50,000	☐ $50,001 to $100,000	☐ $100,001 to $500,000	☐ $500,001 to $1 million	☐ $1,000,001 to $10 million	☐ $10,000,001 to $50 million	☐ $50,000,001 to $100 million	☐ $100,000,001 to $500 million	☐ $500,000,001 to $1 billion	☐ More than $1 billion

B1 (Official Form 1) (4/10)   Page 2

Voluntary Petition *(This page must be completed and filed in every case.)*	Name of Debtor(s)	
All Prior Bankruptcy Cases Filed Within Last 8 Years (If more than two, attach additional sheet.)		
Location Where Filed:	Case Number:	Date Filed:
Location Where Filed:	Case Number:	Date Filed:
Pending Bankruptcy Case Filed by any Spouse, Partner, or Affiliate of this Debtor (If more than one, attach additional sheet.)		
Name of Debtor:	Case Number:	Date Filed:
District:	Relationship:	Judge:

Exhibit A	**Exhibit B**
(To be completed if debtor is required to file periodic reports (e.g., forms 10K and 10Q) with the Securities and Exchange Commission pursuant to Section 13 or 15(d) of the Securities Exchange Act of 1934 and is requesting relief under chapter 11.)	(To be completed if debtor is an individual whose debts are primarily consumer debts.) I, the attorney for the petitioner named in the foregoing petition, declare that I have informed the petitioner that [he or she] may proceed under chapter 7, 11, 12, or 13 of title 11, United States Code, and have explained the relief available under each such chapter. I further certify that I have delivered to the debtor the notice required by 11 U.S.C. § 342(b).
☐ Exhibit A is attached and made a part of this petition.	X _____
	Signature of Attorney for Debtor(s) (Date)

Exhibit C

Does the debtor own or have possession of any property that poses or is alleged to pose a threat of imminent and identifiable harm to public health or safety?

☐   Yes, and Exhibit C is attached and made a part of this petition.

☐   No.

Exhibit D

(To be completed by every individual debtor. If a joint petition is filed, each spouse must complete and attach a separate Exhibit D.)

☐   Exhibit D completed and signed by the debtor is attached and made a part of this petition.

If this is a joint petition:

☐   Exhibit D also completed and signed by the joint debtor is attached and made a part of this petition.

Information Regarding the Debtor - Venue
(Check any applicable box.)

☐   Debtor has been domiciled or has had a residence, principal place of business, or principal assets in this District for 180 days immediately preceding the date of this petition or for a longer part of such 180 days than in any other District.

☐   There is a bankruptcy case concerning debtor's affiliate, general partner, or partnership pending in this District.

☐   Debtor is a debtor in a foreign proceeding and has its principal place of business or principal assets in the United States in this District, or has no principal place of business or assets in the United States but is a defendant in an action or proceeding [in a federal or state court] in this District, or the interests of the parties will be served in regard to the relief sought in this District.

Certification by a Debtor Who Resides as a Tenant of Residential Property
(Check all applicable boxes.)

☐   Landlord has a judgment against the debtor for possession of debtor's residence. (If box checked, complete the following.)

_____
(Name of landlord that obtained judgment)

_____
(Address of landlord)

☐   Debtor claims that under applicable nonbankruptcy law, there are circumstances under which the debtor would be permitted to cure the entire monetary default that gave rise to the judgment for possession, after the judgment for possession was entered, and

☐   Debtor has included with this petition the deposit with the court of any rent that would become due during the 30-day period after the filing of the petition.

☐   Debtor certifies that he/she has served the Landlord with this certification. (11 U.S.C. § 362(l)).

B1 (Official Form) 1 (4/10)   Page 3

Voluntary Petition *(This page must be completed and filed in every case.)*	Name of Debtor(s):

Signatures	
Signature(s) of Debtor(s) (Individual/Joint)	**Signature of a Foreign Representative**

<table>
<tr>
<td>

I declare under penalty of perjury that the information provided in this petition is true and correct.
[If petitioner is an individual whose debts are primarily consumer debts and has chosen to file under chapter 7] I am aware that I may proceed under chapter 7, 11, 12 or 13 of title 11, United States Code, understand the relief available under each such chapter, and choose to proceed under chapter 7.
[If no attorney represents me and no bankruptcy petition preparer signs the petition] I have obtained and read the notice required by 11 U.S.C. § 342(b).

I request relief in accordance with the chapter of title 11, United States Code, specified in this petition.

X _____
   Signature of Debtor

X _____
   Signature of Joint Debtor

_____
Telephone Number (if not represented by attorney)

_____
Date

</td>
<td>

I declare under penalty of perjury that the information provided in this petition is true and correct, that I am the foreign representative of a debtor in a foreign proceeding, and that I am authorized to file this petition.

(Check only one box.)

☐   I request relief in accordance with chapter 15 of title 11, United States Code. Certified copies of the documents required by 11 U.S.C. § 1515 are attached.

☐   Pursuant to 11 U.S.C. § 1511, I request relief in accordance with the chapter of title 11 specified in this petition. A certified copy of the order granting recognition of the foreign main proceeding is attached.

X _____
   (Signature of Foreign Representative)

_____
   (Printed Name of Foreign Representative)

_____
Date

</td>
</tr>
<tr>
<td>Signature of Attorney*</td>
<td>Signature of Non-Attorney Bankruptcy Petition Preparer</td>
</tr>
<tr>
<td>

X _____
   Signature of Attorney for Debtor(s)

_____
Printed Name of Attorney for Debtor(s)

_____
Firm Name

_____
Address

_____
Telephone Number

_____
Date

*In a case in which § 707(b)(4)(D) applies, this signature also constitutes a certification that the attorney has no knowledge after an inquiry that the information in the schedules is incorrect.

</td>
<td rowspan="2">

I declare under penalty of perjury that: (1) I am a bankruptcy petition preparer as defined in 11 U.S.C. § 110; (2) I prepared this document for compensation and have provided the debtor with a copy of this document and the notices and information required under 11 U.S.C. §§ 110(b), 110(h), and 342(b); and, (3) if rules or guidelines have been promulgated pursuant to 11 U.S.C. § 110(h) setting a maximum fee for services chargeable by bankruptcy petition preparers, I have given the debtor notice of the maximum amount before preparing any document for filing for a debtor or accepting any fee from the debtor, as required in that section. Official Form 19 is attached.

_____
Printed Name and title, if any, of Bankruptcy Petition Preparer

_____
Social-Security number (If the bankruptcy petition preparer is not an individual, state the Social-Security number of the officer, principal, responsible person or partner of the bankruptcy petition preparer.) (Required by 11 U.S.C. § 110.)

X _____
   Address

_____
Date

Signature of bankruptcy petition preparer or officer, principal, responsible person, or partner whose Social-Security number is provided above.

Names and Social-Security numbers of all other individuals who prepared or assisted in preparing this document unless the bankruptcy petition preparer is not an individual.

If more than one person prepared this document, attach additional sheets conforming to the appropriate official form for each person.

A bankruptcy petition preparer's failure to comply with the provisions of title 11 and the Federal Rules of Bankruptcy Procedure may result in fines or imprisonment or both. 11 U.S.C. § 110; 18 U.S.C. § 156.

</td>
</tr>
<tr>
<td>

Signature of Debtor (Corporation/Partnership)

I declare under penalty of perjury that the information provided in this petition is true and correct, and that I have been authorized to file this petition on behalf of the debtor.

The debtor requests the relief in accordance with the chapter of title 11, United States Code, specified in this petition.

X _____
   Signature of Authorized Individual

_____
Printed Name of Authorized Individual

_____
Title of Authorized Individual

_____
Date

</td>
</tr>
</table>

APPENDIX B

B6–SUMMARY OF SCHEDULES

B6 Summary (Official Form 6 - Summary) (12/07)

United States Bankruptcy Court

In re _____.
      Debtor

Case No. _____

Chapter _____

SUMMARY OF SCHEDULES

Indicate as to each schedule whether that schedule is attached and state the number of pages in each. Report the totals from Schedules A. B. D. E. F. I. and J in the boxes provided. Add the amounts from Schedules A and B to determine the total amount of the debtor's assets. Add the amounts of all claims from Schedules D, E, and F to determine the total amount of the debtor's liabilities. Individual debtors also must complete the "Statistical Summary of Certain Liabilities and Related Data" if they file a case under chapter 7, 11, or 13.

NAME OF SCHEDULE	ATTACHED (YES/NO)	NO. OF SHEETS	ASSETS	LIABILITIES	OTHER
A - Real Property			$		
B - Personal Property			$		
C - Property Claimed as Exempt					
D - Creditors Holding Secured Claims				$	
E - Creditors Holding Unsecured Priority Claims (Total of Claims on Schedule E)				$	
F - Creditors Holding Unsecured Nonpriority Claims				$	
G - Executory Contracts and Unexpired Leases					
H - Codebtors					
I - Current Income of Individual Debtor(s)					$
J - Current Expenditures of Individual Debtor(s)					$
TOTAL			$	$	

B 6 Summary (Official Form 6 - Summary) (12/07)

United States Bankruptcy Court

In re _____ .   Case No. _____
                    Debtor
                                    Chapter _____

STATISTICAL SUMMARY OF CERTAIN LIABILITIES AND RELATED DATA (28 U.S.C. § 159)

If you are an individual debtor whose debts are primarily consumer debts, as defined in § 101(8) of the Bankruptcy Code (11 U.S.C. § 101(8)), filing a case under chapter 7, 11 or 13, you must report all information requested below.

☐ Check this box if you are an individual debtor whose debts are NOT primarily consumer debts. You are not required to report any information here.

This information is for statistical purposes only under 28 U.S.C. § 159.

Summarize the following types of liabilities, as reported in the Schedules, and total them.

Type of Liability	Amount
Domestic Support Obligations (from Schedule E)	$
Taxes and Certain Other Debts Owed to Governmental Units (from Schedule E)	$
Claims for Death or Personal Injury While Debtor Was Intoxicated (from Schedule E) (whether disputed or undisputed)	$
Student Loan Obligations (from Schedule F)	$
Domestic Support, Separation Agreement, and Divorce Decree Obligations Not Reported on Schedule E	$
Obligations to Pension or Profit-Sharing, and Other Similar Obligations (from Schedule F)	$
TOTAL	$

State the following:

Average Income (from Schedule I, Line 16)	$
Average Expenses (from Schedule J, Line 18)	$
Current Monthly Income (from Form 22A Line 12; OR, Form 22B Line 11; OR, Form 22C Line 20)	$

State the following:

1. Total from Schedule D, "UNSECURED PORTION, IF ANY" column		$
2. Total from Schedule E, "AMOUNT ENTITLED TO PRIORITY" column.	$	
3. Total from Schedule E, "AMOUNT NOT ENTITLED TO PRIORITY, IF ANY" column		$
4. Total from Schedule F		$
5. Total of non-priority unsecured debt (sum of 1, 3, and 4)		$

APPENDIX C

B6 SCHEDULE A–REAL PROPERTY

B6A (Official Form 6A) (12/07)

In re _____,   **Case No.** _____
        Debtor   (If known)

SCHEDULE A - REAL PROPERTY

Except as directed below, list all real property in which the debtor has any legal, equitable, or future interest, including all property owned as a co-tenant, community property, or in which the debtor has a life estate. Include any property in which the debtor holds rights and powers exercisable for the debtor's own benefit. If the debtor is married, state whether the husband, wife, both, or the marital community own the property by placing an "H," "W," "J," or "C" in the column labeled "Husband, Wife, Joint, or Community." If the debtor holds no interest in real property, write "None" under "Description and Location of Property."

Do not include interests in executory contracts and unexpired leases on this schedule. List them in Schedule G - Executory Contracts and Unexpired Leases.

If an entity claims to have a lien or hold a secured interest in any property, state the amount of the secured claim. See Schedule D. If no entity claims to hold a secured interest in the property, write "None" in the column labeled "Amount of Secured Claim."

If the debtor is an individual or if a joint petition is filed, state the amount of any exemption claimed in the property only in Schedule C - Property Claimed as Exempt.

DESCRIPTION AND LOCATION OF PROPERTY	NATURE OF DEBTOR'S INTEREST IN PROPERTY	HUSBAND, WIFE, JOINT, OR COMMUNITY	CURRENT VALUE OF DEBTOR'S INTEREST IN PROPERTY, WITHOUT DEDUCTING ANY SECURED CLAIM OR EXEMPTION	AMOUNT OF SECURED CLAIM

Total▶

(Report also on Summary of Schedules.)

APPENDIX D

B6 SCHEDULE B–PERSONAL PROPERTY

B 6B (Official Form 6B) (12/07)

In re _____,   Case No. _____
                Debtor   **(If known)**

SCHEDULE B - PERSONAL PROPERTY

Except as directed below, list all personal property of the debtor of whatever kind. If the debtor has no property in one or more of the categories, place an "x" in the appropriate position in the column labeled "None." If additional space is needed in any category, attach a separate sheet properly identified with the case name, case number, and the number of the category. If the debtor is married, state whether the husband, wife, both, or the marital community own the property by placing an "H," "W," "J," or "C" in the column labeled "Husband, Wife, Joint, or Community." If the debtor is an individual or a joint petition is filed, state the amount of any exemptions claimed only in Schedule C - Property Claimed as Exempt.

Do not list interests in executory contracts and unexpired leases on this schedule. List them in Schedule G - Executory Contracts and Unexpired Leases.

If the property is being held for the debtor by someone else, state that person's name and address under "Description and Location of Property." If the property is being held for a minor child, simply state the child's initials and the name and address of the child's parent or guardian, such as "A.B., a minor child, by John Doe, guardian." Do not disclose the child's name. See. 11 U.S.C. §112 and Fed. R. Bankr. P. 1007(m).

TYPE OF PROPERTY	N O N E	DESCRIPTION AND LOCATION OF PROPERTY	HUSBAND, WIFE, JOINT, OR COMMUNITY	CURRENT VALUE OF DEBTOR'S INTEREST IN PROPERTY, WITH-OUT DEDUCTING ANY SECURED CLAIM OR EXEMPTION
1. Cash on hand.				
2. Checking, savings or other financial accounts, certificates of deposit or shares in banks, savings and loan, thrift, building and loan, and homestead associations, or credit unions, brokerage houses, or cooperatives.				
3. Security deposits with public utilities, telephone companies, landlords, and others.				
4. Household goods and furnishings, including audio, video, and computer equipment.				
5. Books; pictures and other art objects; antiques; stamp, coin, record, tape, compact disc, and other collections or collectibles.				
6. Wearing apparel.				
7. Furs and jewelry.				
8. Firearms and sports, photographic, and other hobby equipment.				
9. Interests in insurance policies. Name insurance company of each policy and itemize surrender or refund value of each.				
10. Annuities. Itemize and name each issuer.				
11. Interests in an education IRA as defined in 26 U.S.C. § 530(b)(1) or under a qualified State tuition plan as defined in 26 U.S.C. § 529(b)(1). Give particulars. (File separately the record(s) of any such interest(s). 11 U.S.C. § 521(c).)				

B 6B (Official Form 6B) (12/07) -- Cont.

In re _____ ,   Case No. _____
            Debtor   **(If known)**

SCHEDULE B - PERSONAL PROPERTY
(Continuation Sheet)

TYPE OF PROPERTY	N O N E	DESCRIPTION AND LOCATION OF PROPERTY	HUSBAND, WIFE, JOINT, OR COMMUNITY	CURRENT VALUE OF DEBTOR'S INTEREST IN PROPERTY, WITH- OUT DEDUCTING ANY SECURED CLAIM OR EXEMPTION
12. Interests in IRA, ERISA, Keogh, or other pension or profit sharing plans. Give particulars.				
13. Stock and interests in incorporated and unincorporated businesses. Itemize.				
14. Interests in partnerships or joint ventures. Itemize.				
15. Government and corporate bonds and other negotiable and non-negotiable instruments.				
16. Accounts receivable.				
17. Alimony, maintenance, support, and property settlements to which the debtor is or may be entitled. Give particulars.				
18. Other liquidated debts owed to debtor including tax refunds. Give particulars.				
19. Equitable or future interests, life estates, and rights or powers exercisable for the benefit of the debtor other than those listed in Schedule A – Real Property.				
20. Contingent and noncontingent interests in estate of a decedent, death benefit plan, life insurance policy, or trust.				
21. Other contingent and unliquidated claims of every nature, including tax refunds, counterclaims of the debtor, and rights to setoff claims. Give estimated value of each.				

B 6B (Official Form 6B) (12/07) -- Cont.

In re _____ ,   Case No. _____
            Debtor   **(If known)**

SCHEDULE B - PERSONAL PROPERTY
(Continuation Sheet)

TYPE OF PROPERTY	NONE	DESCRIPTION AND LOCATION OF PROPERTY	HUSBAND, WIFE, JOINT, OR COMMUNITY	CURRENT VALUE OF DEBTOR'S INTEREST IN PROPERTY, WITHOUT DEDUCTING ANY SECURED CLAIM OR EXEMPTION
22. Patents, copyrights, and other intellectual property. Give particulars.				
23. Licenses, franchises, and other general intangibles. Give particulars.				
24. Customer lists or other compilations containing personally identifiable information (as defined in 11 U.S.C. § 101(41A)) provided to the debtor by individuals in connection with obtaining a product or service from the debtor primarily for personal, family, or household purposes.				
25. Automobiles, trucks, trailers, and other vehicles and accessories.				
26. Boats, motors, and accessories.				
27. Aircraft and accessories.				
28. Office equipment, furnishings, and supplies.				
29. Machinery, fixtures, equipment, and supplies used in business.				
30. Inventory.				
31. Animals.				
32. Crops - growing or harvested. Give particulars.				
33. Farming equipment and implements.				
34. Farm supplies, chemicals, and feed.				
35. Other personal property of any kind not already listed. Itemize.				

_____ continuation sheets attached   Total▶ $

APPENDIX E

B6 SCHEDULE C–EXEMPT PROPERTY

B 6C (Official Form 6C) (04/10)

In re _____,   Case No. _____
            Debtor   (If known)

SCHEDULE C - PROPERTY CLAIMED AS EXEMPT

Debtor claims the exemptions to which debtor is entitled under:
(Check one box)
☐ 11 U.S.C. § 522(b)(2)
☐ 11 U.S.C. § 522(b)(3)

☐ Check if debtor claims a homestead exemption that exceeds $146,450.*

DESCRIPTION OF PROPERTY	SPECIFY LAW PROVIDING EACH EXEMPTION	VALUE OF CLAIMED EXEMPTION	CURRENT VALUE OF PROPERTY WITHOUT DEDUCTING EXEMPTION

* Amount subject to adjustment on 4/1/13, and every three years thereafter with respect to cases commenced on or after the date of adjustment.

APPENDIX F

B6 SCHEDULE D–SECURED CREDITORS

B 6D (Official Form 6D) (12/07)

In re _____ ,   Case No. _____

               Debtor   **(If known)**

SCHEDULE D - CREDITORS HOLDING SECURED CLAIMS

State the name, mailing address, including zip code, and last four digits of any account number of all entities holding claims secured by property of the debtor as of the date of filing of the petition. The complete account number of any account the debtor has with the creditor is useful to the trustee and the creditor and may be provided if the debtor chooses to do so. List creditors holding all types of secured interests such as judgment liens, garnishments, statutory liens, mortgages, deeds of trust, and other security interests.

List creditors in alphabetical order to the extent practicable. If a minor child is the creditor, state the child's initials and the name and address of the child's parent or guardian, such as "A.B., a minor child, by John Doe, guardian." Do not disclose the child's name. See, 11 U.S.C. §112 and Fed. R. Bankr. P. 1007(m). If all secured creditors will not fit on this page, use the continuation sheet provided.

If any entity other than a spouse in a joint case may be jointly liable on a claim, place an "X" in the column labeled "Codebtor," include the entity on the appropriate schedule of creditors, and complete Schedule H – Codebtors. If a joint petition is filed, state whether the husband, wife, both of them, or the marital community may be liable on each claim by placing an "H," "W," "J," or "C" in the column labeled "Husband, Wife, Joint, or Community."

If the claim is contingent, place an "X" in the column labeled "Contingent." If the claim is unliquidated, place an "X" in the column labeled "Unliquidated." If the claim is disputed, place an "X" in the column labeled "Disputed." (You may need to place an "X" in more than one of these three columns.)

Total the columns labeled "Amount of Claim Without Deducting Value of Collateral" and "Unsecured Portion, if Any" in the boxes labeled "Total(s)" on the last sheet of the completed schedule. Report the total from the column labeled "Amount of Claim Without Deducting Value of Collateral" also on the Summary of Schedules and, if the debtor is an individual with primarily consumer debts, report the total from the column labeled "Unsecured Portion, if Any" on the Statistical Summary of Certain Liabilities and Related Data.

☐   Check this box if debtor has no creditors holding secured claims to report on this Schedule D.

CREDITOR'S NAME AND MAILING ADDRESS INCLUDING ZIP CODE AND AN ACCOUNT NUMBER (See Instructions Above.)	CODEBTOR	HUSBAND, WIFE, JOINT, OR COMMUNITY	DATE CLAIM WAS INCURRED, NATURE OF LIEN, AND DESCRIPTION AND VALUE OF PROPERTY SUBJECT TO LIEN	CONTINGENT	UNLIQUIDATED	DISPUTED	AMOUNT OF CLAIM WITHOUT DEDUCTING VALUE OF COLLATERAL	UNSECURED PORTION, IF ANY
ACCOUNT NO.								
			VALUE $					
ACCOUNT NO.								
			VALUE $					
ACCOUNT NO.								
			VALUE $					
___ continuation sheets attached			Subtotal ► (Total of this page)				$	$
			Total ► (Use only on last page)				$	$
							(Report also on Summary of Schedules.)	(If applicable, report also on Statistical Summary of Certain Liabilities and Related Data.)

B 6D (Official Form 6D) (12/07) – Cont.

In re _____.   Case No. _____
         Debtor   **(if known)**

SCHEDULE D - CREDITORS HOLDING SECURED CLAIMS
(Continuation Sheet)

CREDITOR'S NAME AND MAILING ADDRESS INCLUDING ZIP CODE AND AN ACCOUNT NUMBER (See Instructions Above.)	CODEBTOR	HUSBAND, WIFE, JOINT, OR COMMUNITY	DATE CLAIM WAS INCURRED, NATURE OF LIEN , AND DESCRIPTION AND VALUE OF PROPERTY SUBJECT TO LIEN	CONTINGENT	UNLIQUIDATED	DISPUTED	AMOUNT OF CLAIM WITHOUT DEDUCTING VALUE OF COLLATERAL	UNSECURED PORTION, IF ANY
ACCOUNT NO.								
			VALUE $					
ACCOUNT NO.								
			VALUE $					
ACCOUNT NO.								
			VALUE $					
ACCOUNT NO.								
			VALUE $					
ACCOUNT NO.								
			VALUE $					

Sheet no____ of ____ continuation sheets attached to Schedule of Creditors Holding Secured Claims

Subtotal (s)▶ (Total(s) of this page) $ $

Total(s) ▶ (Use only on last page) $ $

(Report also on Summary of Schedules.)   (If applicable, report also on Statistical Summary of Certain Liabilities and Related Data.)

APPENDIX G

B6 SCHEDULE E–UNSECURED PRIORITY CLAIM

B 6E (Official Form 6E) (04/10)

In re _____,   Case No._____

             Debtor   *(if known)*

SCHEDULE E - CREDITORS HOLDING UNSECURED PRIORITY CLAIMS

A complete list of claims entitled to priority, listed separately by type of priority, is to be set forth on the sheets provided. Only holders of unsecured claims entitled to priority should be listed in this schedule. In the boxes provided on the attached sheets, state the name, mailing address, including zip code, and last four digits of the account number, if any, of all entities holding priority claims against the debtor or the property of the debtor, as of the date of the filing of the petition. Use a separate continuation sheet for each type of priority and label each with the type of priority.

The complete account number of any account the debtor has with the creditor is useful to the trustee and the creditor and may be provided if the debtor chooses to do so. If a minor child is a creditor, state the child's initials and the name and address of the child's parent or guardian, such as "A.B., a minor child, by John Doe, guardian." Do not disclose the child's name. See, 11 U.S.C. §112 and Fed. R. Bankr. P. 1007(m).

If any entity other than a spouse in a joint case may be jointly liable on a claim, place an "X" in the column labeled "Codebtor," include the entity on the appropriate schedule of creditors, and complete Schedule H-Codebtors. If a joint petition is filed, state whether the husband, wife, both of them, or the marital community may be liable on each claim by placing an "H," "W," "J," or "C" in the column labeled "Husband, Wife, Joint, or Community." If the claim is contingent, place an "X" in the column labeled "Contingent." If the claim is unliquidated, place an "X" in the column labeled "Unliquidated." If the claim is disputed, place an "X" in the column labeled "Disputed." (You may need to place an "X" in more than one of these three columns.)

Report the total of claims listed on each sheet in the box labeled "Subtotals" on each sheet. Report the total of all claims listed on this Schedule E in the box labeled "Total" on the last sheet of the completed schedule. Report this total also on the Summary of Schedules.

Report the total of amounts entitled to priority listed on each sheet in the box labeled "Subtotals" on each sheet. Report the total of all amounts entitled to priority listed on this Schedule E in the box labeled "Totals" on the last sheet of the completed schedule. Individual debtors with primarily consumer debts report this total also on the Statistical Summary of Certain Liabilities and Related Data.

Report the total of amounts **not** entitled to priority listed on each sheet in the box labeled "Subtotals" on each sheet. Report the total of all amounts not entitled to priority listed on this Schedule E in the box labeled "Totals" on the last sheet of the completed schedule. Individual debtors with primarily consumer debts report this total also on the Statistical Summary of Certain Liabilities and Related Data.

☐   Check this box if debtor has no creditors holding unsecured priority claims to report on this Schedule E.

TYPES OF PRIORITY CLAIMS (Check the appropriate box(es) below if claims in that category are listed on the attached sheets.)

☐ **Domestic Support Obligations**

Claims for domestic support that are owed to or recoverable by a spouse, former spouse, or child of the debtor, or the parent, legal guardian, or responsible relative of such a child, or a governmental unit to whom such a domestic support claim has been assigned to the extent provided in 11 U.S.C. § 507(a)(1).

☐ **Extensions of credit in an involuntary case**

Claims arising in the ordinary course of the debtor's business or financial affairs after the commencement of the case but before the earlier of the appointment of a trustee or the order for relief. 11 U.S.C. § 507(a)(3).

☐ **Wages, salaries, and commissions**

Wages, salaries, and commissions, including vacation, severance, and sick leave pay owing to employees and commissions owing to qualifying independent sales representatives up to $11,725* per person earned within 180 days immediately preceding the filing of the original petition, or the cessation of business, whichever occurred first, to the extent provided in 11 U.S.C. § 507(a)(4).

☐ **Contributions to employee benefit plans**

Money owed to employee benefit plans for services rendered within 180 days immediately preceding the filing of the original petition, or the cessation of business, whichever occurred first, to the extent provided in 11 U.S.C. § 507(a)(5).

---

* *Amount subject to adjustment on 4/01/13, and every three years thereafter with respect to cases commenced on or after the date of adjustment.*

B 6E (Official Form 6E) (04/10) – Cont.

In re _____ ,   Case No._____
                    Debtor   (if known)

☐ **Certain farmers and fishermen**

  Claims of certain farmers and fishermen, up to $5,775* per farmer or fisherman, against the debtor, as provided in 11 U.S.C. § 507(a)(6).

☐ **Deposits by individuals**

  Claims of individuals up to $2,600* for deposits for the purchase, lease, or rental of property or services for personal, family, or household use, that were not delivered or provided. 11 U.S.C. § 507(a)(7).

☐ **Taxes and Certain Other Debts Owed to Governmental Units**

  Taxes, customs duties, and penalties owing to federal, state, and local governmental units as set forth in 11 U.S.C. § 507(a)(8).

☐ **Commitments to Maintain the Capital of an Insured Depository Institution**

  Claims based on commitments to the FDIC, RTC, Director of the Office of Thrift Supervision, Comptroller of the Currency, or Board of Governors of the Federal Reserve System, or their predecessors or successors, to maintain the capital of an insured depository institution. 11 U.S.C. § 507 (a)(9).

☐ **Claims for Death or Personal Injury While Debtor Was Intoxicated**

  Claims for death or personal injury resulting from the operation of a motor vehicle or vessel while the debtor was intoxicated from using alcohol, a drug, or another substance. 11 U.S.C. § 507(a)(10).

* *Amounts are subject to adjustment on 4/01/13, and every three years thereafter with respect to cases commenced on or after the date of adjustment.*

_____ continuation sheets attached

B 6E (Official Form 6E) (04/10) – Cont.

In re _____,   Case No. _____
    Debtor   **(if known)**

SCHEDULE E - CREDITORS HOLDING UNSECURED PRIORITY CLAIMS
(Continuation Sheet)

Type of Priority for Claims Listed on This Sheet

CREDITOR'S NAME, MAILING ADDRESS INCLUDING ZIP CODE, AND ACCOUNT NUMBER (See instructions above.)	CODEBTOR	HUSBAND, WIFE, JOINT, OR COMMUNITY	DATE CLAIM WAS INCURRED AND CONSIDERATION FOR CLAIM	CONTINGENT	UNLIQUIDATED	DISPUTED	AMOUNT OF CLAIM	AMOUNT ENTITLED TO PRIORITY	AMOUNT NOT ENTITLED TO PRIORITY, IF ANY
Account No.									
Account No.									
Account No.									
Account No.									

Sheet no. ___ of ___ continuation sheets attached to Schedule of Creditors Holding Priority Claims

Subtotals▶ (Totals of this page) $ $

Total▶ (Use only on last page of the completed Schedule E. Report also on the Summary of Schedules.) $

Totals▶ (Use only on last page of the completed Schedule E. If applicable, report also on the Statistical Summary of Certain Liabilities and Related Data.) $ $

APPENDIX H

B6 SCHEDULE F–UNSECURED CREDITORS

B 6F (Official Form 6F) (12/07)

In re _____.   **Case No.** _____
                    Debtor   (if known)

SCHEDULE F - CREDITORS HOLDING UNSECURED NONPRIORITY CLAIMS

State the name, mailing address, including zip code, and last four digits of any account number, of all entities holding unsecured claims without priority against the debtor or the property of the debtor, as of the date of filing of the petition. The complete account number of any account the debtor has with the creditor is useful to the trustee and the creditor and may be provided if the debtor chooses to do so. If a minor child is a creditor, state the child's initials and the name and address of the child's parent or guardian, such as "A.B., a minor child, by John Doe, guardian." Do not disclose the child's name. See, 11 U.S.C. §112 and Fed. R. Bankr. P. 1007(m). Do not include claims listed in Schedules D and E. If all creditors will not fit on this page, use the continuation sheet provided.

If any entity other than a spouse in a joint case may be jointly liable on a claim, place an "X" in the column labeled "Codebtor," include the entity on the appropriate schedule of creditors, and complete Schedule H - Codebtors. If a joint petition is filed, state whether the husband, wife, both of them, or the marital community may be liable on each claim by placing an "H," "W," "J," or "C" in the column labeled "Husband, Wife, Joint, or Community."

If the claim is contingent, place an "X" in the column labeled "Contingent." If the claim is unliquidated, place an "X" in the column labeled "Unliquidated." If the claim is disputed, place an "X" in the column labeled "Disputed." (You may need to place an "X" in more than one of these three columns.)

Report the total of all claims listed on this schedule in the box labeled "Total" on the last sheet of the completed schedule. Report this total also on the Summary of Schedules and, if the debtor is an individual with primarily consumer debts, report this total also on the Statistical Summary of Certain Liabilities and Related Data.

☐   Check this box if debtor has no creditors holding unsecured claims to report on this Schedule F.

CREDITOR'S NAME, MAILING ADDRESS INCLUDING ZIP CODE, AND ACCOUNT NUMBER (See instructions above.)	CODEBTOR	HUSBAND, WIFE, JOINT, OR COMMUNITY	DATE CLAIM WAS INCURRED AND CONSIDERATION FOR CLAIM. IF CLAIM IS SUBJECT TO SETOFF, SO STATE.	CONTINGENT	UNLIQUIDATED	DISPUTED	AMOUNT OF CLAIM
ACCOUNT NO.							
ACCOUNT NO.							
ACCOUNT NO.							
ACCOUNT NO.							
			Subtotal▶				$
_____ continuation sheets attached			Total▶ (Use only on last page of the completed Schedule F.) (Report also on Summary of Schedules and, if applicable, on the Statistical Summary of Certain Liabilities and Related Data.)				$

B 6F (Official Form 6F) (12/07) - Cont.

In re _____,   Case No. _____
                    Debtor   **(if known)**

SCHEDULE F - CREDITORS HOLDING UNSECURED NONPRIORITY CLAIMS
(Continuation Sheet)

CREDITOR'S NAME, MAILING ADDRESS INCLUDING ZIP CODE, AND ACCOUNT NUMBER (See instructions above.)	CODEBTOR	HUSBAND, WIFE, JOINT, OR COMMUNITY	DATE CLAIM WAS INCURRED AND CONSIDERATION FOR CLAIM. IF CLAIM IS SUBJECT TO SETOFF, SO STATE.	CONTINGENT	UNLIQUIDATED	DISPUTED	AMOUNT OF CLAIM
ACCOUNT NO.							
ACCOUNT NO.							
ACCOUNT NO.							
ACCOUNT NO.							
ACCOUNT NO.							

Sheet no. ____ of ____ continuation sheets attached
to Schedule of Creditors Holding Unsecured
Nonpriority Claims

Subtotal▶ $

Total▶ $
(Use only on last page of the completed Schedule F.)
(Report also on Summary of Schedules and, if applicable on the Statistical
Summary of Certain Liabilities and Related Data.)

APPENDIX I

B6 SCHEDULE G–UNEXPIRED LEASES AND EXECUTORY CONTRACTS

B 6G (Official Form 6G) (12/07)

In re _____ ,   Case No._____
             Debtor   **(if known)**

SCHEDULE G - EXECUTORY CONTRACTS AND UNEXPIRED LEASES

Describe all executory contracts of any nature and all unexpired leases of real or personal property. Include any timeshare interests. State nature of debtor's interest in contract, i.e., "Purchaser," "Agent," etc. State whether debtor is the lessor or lessee of a lease. Provide the names and complete mailing addresses of all other parties to each lease or contract described. If a minor child is a party to one of the leases or contracts, state the child's initials and the name and address of the child's parent or guardian, such as "A.B., a minor child, by John Doe, guardian." Do not disclose the child's name. See, 11 U.S.C. §112 and Fed. R. Bankr. P. 1007(m).

☐ Check this box if debtor has no executory contracts or unexpired leases.

NAME AND MAILING ADDRESS, INCLUDING ZIP CODE, OF OTHER PARTIES TO LEASE OR CONTRACT.	DESCRIPTION OF CONTRACT OR LEASE AND NATURE OF DEBTOR'S INTEREST. STATE WHETHER LEASE IS FOR NONRESIDENTIAL REAL PROPERTY. STATE CONTRACT NUMBER OF ANY GOVERNMENT CONTRACT.

APPENDIX J

B6 SCHEDULE H–CO-DEBTORS

B 6H (Official Form 6H) (12/07)

In re _____ ,   Case No. _____
            Debtor   **(if known)**

SCHEDULE H - CODEBTORS

Provide the information requested concerning any person or entity, other than a spouse in a joint case, that is also liable on any debts listed by the debtor in the schedules of creditors. Include all guarantors and co-signers. If the debtor resides or resided in a community property state, commonwealth, or territory (including Alaska, Arizona, California, Idaho, Louisiana, Nevada, New Mexico, Puerto Rico, Texas, Washington, or Wisconsin) within the eight-year period immediately preceding the commencement of the case, identify the name of the debtor's spouse and of any former spouse who resides or resided with the debtor in the community property state, commonwealth, or territory. Include all names used by the nondebtor spouse during the eight years immediately preceding the commencement of this case. If a minor child is a codebtor or a creditor, state the child's initials and the name and address of the child's parent or guardian, such as "A.B., a minor child, by John Doe, guardian." Do not disclose the child's name. See. 11 U.S.C. §112 and Fed. R. Bankr. P. 1007(m).

☐ Check this box if debtor has no codebtors.

NAME AND ADDRESS OF CODEBTOR	NAME AND ADDRESS OF CREDITOR

APPENDIX K

B6 SCHEDULE I–INCOME

B6I (Official Form 6I) (12/07)

In re _____,   Case No. _____
      Debtor   **(if known)**

SCHEDULE I - CURRENT INCOME OF INDIVIDUAL DEBTOR(S)

The column labeled "Spouse" must be completed in all cases filed by joint debtors and by every married debtor, whether or not a joint petition is filed, unless the spouses are separated and a joint petition is not filed. Do not state the name of any minor child. The average monthly income calculated on this form may differ from the current monthly income calculated on Form 22A, 22B, or 22C.

Debtor's Marital Status:	DEPENDENTS OF DEBTOR AND SPOUSE	
	RELATIONSHIP(S):	AGE(S):

Employment:	DEBTOR	SPOUSE
Occupation		
Name of Employer		
How long employed		
Address of Employer		

INCOME: (Estimate of average or projected monthly income at time case filed)

	DEBTOR	SPOUSE
1. Monthly gross wages, salary, and commissions (Prorate if not paid monthly)	$_____	$_____
2. Estimate monthly overtime	$_____	$_____
3. SUBTOTAL	$_____	$_____
4. LESS PAYROLL DEDUCTIONS		
a. Payroll taxes and social security	$_____	$_____
b. Insurance	$_____	$_____
c. Union dues	$_____	$_____
d. Other (Specify): _____	$_____	$_____
5. SUBTOTAL OF PAYROLL DEDUCTIONS	$_____	$_____
6. TOTAL NET MONTHLY TAKE HOME PAY	$_____	$_____
7. Regular income from operation of business or profession or farm (Attach detailed statement)	$_____	$_____
8. Income from real property	$_____	$_____
9. Interest and dividends	$_____	$_____
10. Alimony, maintenance or support payments payable to the debtor for the debtor's use or that of dependents listed above	$_____	$_____
11. Social security or government assistance (Specify): _____	$_____	$_____
12. Pension or retirement income	$_____	$_____
13. Other monthly income (Specify): _____	$_____	$_____
14. SUBTOTAL OF LINES 7 THROUGH 13	$_____	$_____
15. AVERAGE MONTHLY INCOME (Add amounts on lines 6 and 14)	$_____	$_____
16. COMBINED AVERAGE MONTHLY INCOME: (Combine column totals from line 15)	$_____	

(Report also on Summary of Schedules and, if applicable, on Statistical Summary of Certain Liabilities and Related Data)

17. Describe any increase or decrease in income reasonably anticipated to occur within the year following the filing of this document:

APPENDIX L

B6 SCHEDULE J–EXPENSES

B6J (Official Form 6J) (12/07)

In re _____ .   Case No. _____

 Debtor   (if known)

SCHEDULE J - CURRENT EXPENDITURES OF INDIVIDUAL DEBTOR(S)

Complete this schedule by estimating the average or projected monthly expenses of the debtor and the debtor's family at time case filed. Prorate any payments made bi-weekly, quarterly, semi-annually, or annually to show monthly rate. The average monthly expenses calculated on this form may differ from the deductions from income allowed on Form22A or 22C.

☐ Check this box if a joint petition is filed and debtor's spouse maintains a separate household. Complete a separate schedule of expenditures labeled "Spouse."

1. Rent or home mortgage payment (include lot rented for mobile home) .... $ _____
   a. Are real estate taxes included?   Yes _____   No _____
   b. Is property insurance included?   Yes _____   No _____
2. Utilities: a. Electricity and heating fuel .... $ _____
    b. Water and sewer .... $ _____
    c. Telephone .... $ _____
    d. Other .... $ _____
3. Home maintenance (repairs and upkeep) .... $ _____
4. Food .... $ _____
5. Clothing .... $ _____
6. Laundry and dry cleaning .... $ _____
7. Medical and dental expenses .... $ _____
8. Transportation (not including car payments) .... $ _____
9. Recreation, clubs and entertainment, newspapers, magazines, etc .... $ _____
10. Charitable contributions .... $ _____
11. Insurance (not deducted from wages or included in home mortgage payments)
    a. Homeowner's or renter's .... $ _____
    b. Life .... $ _____
    c. Health .... $ _____
    d. Auto .... $ _____
    e. Other .... $ _____
12. Taxes (not deducted from wages or included in home mortgage payments)
(Specify) .... $ _____
13. Installment payments: (In chapter 11, 12 and 13 cases, do not list payments to be included in the plan)
    a. Auto .... $ _____
    b. Other .... $ _____
    c. Other .... $ _____
14. Alimony, maintenance, and support paid to others .... $ _____
15. Payments for support of additional dependents not living at your home .... $ _____
16. Regular expenses from operation of business, profession, or farm (attach detailed statement) $ _____
17. Other .... $ _____

18. AVERAGE MONTHLY EXPENSES (Total lines 1-17. Report also on Summary of Schedules and,
if applicable, on the Statistical Summary of Certain Liabilities and Related Data.) | $ _____ |

19. Describe any increase or decrease in expenditures reasonably anticipated to occur within the year following the filing of this document:

20. STATEMENT OF MONTHLY NET INCOME:
   a. Average monthly income from Line 15 of Schedule I .... $ _____
   b. Average monthly expenses from Line 18 above .... $ _____
   c. Monthly net income (a. minus b.) .... $ _____

APPENDIX M

B7–STATEMENT OF FINANCIAL AFFAIRS

B 7 (Official Form 7) (04/10)

UNITED STATES BANKRUPTCY COURT

In re:_____,   Case No. _____
                    Debtor   (if known)

STATEMENT OF FINANCIAL AFFAIRS

This statement is to be completed by every debtor. Spouses filing a joint petition may file a single statement on which the information for both spouses is combined. If the case is filed under chapter 12 or chapter 13, a married debtor must furnish information for both spouses whether or not a joint petition is filed, unless the spouses are separated and a joint petition is not filed. An individual debtor engaged in business as a sole proprietor, partner, family farmer, or self-employed professional, should provide the information requested on this statement concerning all such activities as well as the individual's personal affairs. To indicate payments, transfers and the like to minor children, state the child's initials and the name and address of the child's parent or guardian, such as "A.B., a minor child, by John Doe, guardian." Do not disclose the child's name. See, 11 U.S.C. §112 and Fed. R. Bankr. P. 1007(m).

Questions 1 - 18 are to be completed by all debtors. Debtors that are or have been in business, as defined below, also must complete Questions 19 - 25. **If the answer to an applicable question is "None," mark the box labeled "None."** If additional space is needed for the answer to any question, use and attach a separate sheet properly identified with the case name, case number (if known), and the number of the question.

DEFINITIONS

"In business." A debtor is "in business" for the purpose of this form if the debtor is a corporation or partnership. An individual debtor is "in business" for the purpose of this form if the debtor is or has been, within six years immediately preceding the filing of this bankruptcy case, any of the following: an officer, director, managing executive, or owner of 5 percent or more of the voting or equity securities of a corporation; a partner, other than a limited partner, of a partnership; a sole proprietor or self-employed full-time or part-time. An individual debtor also may be "in business" for the purpose of this form if the debtor engages in a trade, business, or other activity, other than as an employee, to supplement income from the debtor's primary employment.

"Insider." The term "insider" includes but is not limited to: relatives of the debtor; general partners of the debtor and their relatives; corporations of which the debtor is an officer, director, or person in control; officers, directors, and any owner of 5 percent or more of the voting or equity securities of a corporate debtor and their relatives; affiliates of the debtor and insiders of such affiliates; any managing agent of the debtor. 11 U.S.C. § 101.

---

1.   Income from employment or operation of business

None
☐

State the gross amount of income the debtor has received from employment, trade, or profession, or from operation of the debtor's business, including part-time activities either as an employee or in independent trade or business, from the beginning of this calendar year to the date this case was commenced. State also the gross amounts received during the **two years** immediately preceding this calendar year. (A debtor that maintains, or has maintained, financial records on the basis of a fiscal rather than a calendar year may report fiscal year income. Identify the beginning and ending dates of the debtor's fiscal year.) If a joint petition is filed, state income for each spouse separately. (Married debtors filing under chapter 12 or chapter 13 must state income of both spouses whether or not a joint petition is filed, unless the spouses are separated and a joint petition is not filed.)

                    AMOUNT   SOURCE

2

2. Income other than from employment or operation of business

None ☐

State the amount of income received by the debtor other than from employment, trade, profession, operation of the debtor's business during the **two years** immediately preceding the commencement of this case. Give particulars. If a joint petition is filed, state income for each spouse separately. (Married debtors filing under chapter 12 or chapter 13 must state income for each spouse whether or not a joint petition is filed, unless the spouses are separated and a joint petition is not filed.)

AMOUNT   SOURCE

3. Payments to creditors

Complete a. or b., as appropriate, and c.

None ☐

a. *Individual or joint debtor(s) with primarily consumer debts:* List all payments on loans, installment purchases of goods or services, and other debts to any creditor made within **90 days** immediately preceding the commencement of this case unless the aggregate value of all property that constitutes or is affected by such transfer is less than $600. Indicate with an asterisk (*) any payments that were made to a creditor on account of a domestic support obligation or as part of an alternative repayment schedule under a plan by an approved nonprofit budgeting and credit counseling agency. (Married debtors filing under chapter 12 or chapter 13 must include payments by either or both spouses whether or not a joint petition is filed, unless the spouses are separated and a joint petition is not filed.)

NAME AND ADDRESS OF CREDITOR	DATES OF PAYMENTS	AMOUNT PAID	AMOUNT STILL OWING

None ☐

b. *Debtor whose debts are not primarily consumer debts:* List each payment or other transfer to any creditor made within **90 days** immediately preceding the commencement of the case unless the aggregate value of all property that constitutes or is affected by such transfer is less than $5,850*. If the debtor is an individual, indicate with an asterisk (*) any payments that were made to a creditor on account of a domestic support obligation or as part of an alternative repayment schedule under a plan by an approved nonprofit budgeting and credit counseling agency. (Married debtors filing under chapter 12 or chapter 13 must include payments and other transfers by either or both spouses whether or not a joint petition is filed, unless the spouses are separated and a joint petition is not filed.)

NAME AND ADDRESS OF CREDITOR	DATES OF PAYMENTS/ TRANSFERS	AMOUNT PAID OR VALUE OF TRANSFERS	AMOUNT STILL OWING

Amount subject to adjustment on 4/01/13, and every three years thereafter with respect to cases commenced on or after the date of adjustment.

3

None

☐ c. *All debtors:* List all payments made within **one year** immediately preceding the commencement of this case to or for the benefit of creditors who are or were insiders. (Married debtors filing under chapter 12 or chapter 13 must include payments by either or both spouses whether or not a joint petition is filed, unless the spouses are separated and a joint petition is not filed.)

NAME AND ADDRESS OF CREDITOR AND RELATIONSHIP TO DEBTOR	DATE OF PAYMENT	AMOUNT PAID	AMOUNT STILL OWING

---

4. Suits and administrative proceedings, executions, garnishments and attachments

None
☐ a. List all suits and administrative proceedings to which the debtor is or was a party within **one year** immediately preceding the filing of this bankruptcy case. (Married debtors filing under chapter 12 or chapter 13 must include information concerning either or both spouses whether or not a joint petition is filed, unless the spouses are separated and a joint petition is not filed.)

CAPTION OF SUIT AND CASE NUMBER	NATURE OF PROCEEDING	COURT OR AGENCY AND LOCATION	STATUS OR DISPOSITION

None
☐ b. Describe all property that has been attached, garnished or seized under any legal or equitable process within **one year** immediately preceding the commencement of this case. (Married debtors filing under chapter 12 or chapter 13 must include information concerning property of either or both spouses whether or not a joint petition is filed, unless the spouses are separated and a joint petition is not filed.)

NAME AND ADDRESS OF PERSON FOR WHOSE BENEFIT PROPERTY WAS SEIZED	DATE OF SEIZURE	DESCRIPTION AND VALUE OF PROPERTY

---

5. Repossessions, foreclosures and returns

None
☐ List all property that has been repossessed by a creditor, sold at a foreclosure sale, transferred through a deed in lieu of foreclosure or returned to the seller, within **one year** immediately preceding the commencement of this case. (Married debtors filing under chapter 12 or chapter 13 must include information concerning property of either or both spouses whether or not a joint petition is filed, unless the spouses are separated and a joint petition is not filed.)

NAME AND ADDRESS OF CREDITOR OR SELLER	DATE OF REPOSSESSION, FORECLOSURE SALE, TRANSFER OR RETURN	DESCRIPTION AND VALUE OF PROPERTY

4

6. Assignments and receiverships

None ☐

a. Describe any assignment of property for the benefit of creditors made within **120 days** immediately preceding the commencement of this case. (Married debtors filing under chapter 12 or chapter 13 must include any assignment by either or both spouses whether or not a joint petition is filed, unless the spouses are separated and a joint petition is not filed.)

NAME AND ADDRESS OF ASSIGNEE	DATE OF ASSIGNMENT	TERMS OF ASSIGNMENT OR SETTLEMENT

None ☐

b. List all property which has been in the hands of a custodian, receiver, or court-appointed official within **one year** immediately preceding the commencement of this case. (Married debtors filing under chapter 12 or chapter 13 must include information concerning property of either or both spouses whether or not a joint petition is filed, unless the spouses are separated and a joint petition is not filed.)

NAME AND ADDRESS OF CUSTODIAN	NAME AND LOCATION OF COURT CASE TITLE & NUMBER	DATE OF ORDER	DESCRIPTION AND VALUE Of PROPERTY

7. Gifts

None ☐

List all gifts or charitable contributions made within **one year** immediately preceding the commencement of this case except ordinary and usual gifts to family members aggregating less than $200 in value per individual family member and charitable contributions aggregating less than $100 per recipient. (Married debtors filing under chapter 12 or chapter 13 must include gifts or contributions by either or both spouses whether or not a joint petition is filed, unless the spouses are separated and a joint petition is not filed.)

NAME AND ADDRESS OF PERSON OR ORGANIZATION	RELATIONSHIP TO DEBTOR, IF ANY	DATE OF GIFT	DESCRIPTION AND VALUE OF GIFT

8. Losses

None ☐

List all losses from fire, theft, other casualty or gambling within **one year** immediately preceding the commencement of this case **or since the commencement of this case**. (Married debtors filing under chapter 12 or chapter 13 must include losses by either or both spouses whether or not a joint petition is filed, unless the spouses are separated and a joint petition is not filed.)

DESCRIPTION AND VALUE OF PROPERTY	DESCRIPTION OF CIRCUMSTANCES AND, IF LOSS WAS COVERED IN WHOLE OR IN PART BY INSURANCE, GIVE PARTICULARS	DATE OF LOSS

5

9. Payments related to debt counseling or bankruptcy

None
☐

List all payments made or property transferred by or on behalf of the debtor to any persons, including attorneys, for consultation concerning debt consolidation, relief under the bankruptcy law or preparation of a petition in bankruptcy within **one year** immediately preceding the commencement of this case.

NAME AND ADDRESS OF PAYEE	DATE OF PAYMENT, NAME OF PAYER IF OTHER THAN DEBTOR	AMOUNT OF MONEY OR DESCRIPTION AND VALUE OF PROPERTY

10. Other transfers

None
☐

a.   List all other property, other than property transferred in the ordinary course of the business or financial affairs of the debtor, transferred either absolutely or as security within **two years** immediately preceding the commencement of this case. (Married debtors filing under chapter 12 or chapter 13 must include transfers by either or both spouses whether or not a joint petition is filed, unless the spouses are separated and a joint petition is not filed.)

NAME AND ADDRESS OF TRANSFEREE, RELATIONSHIP TO DEBTOR	DATE	DESCRIBE PROPERTY TRANSFERRED AND VALUE RECEIVED

None
☐

b.   List all property transferred by the debtor within **ten years** immediately preceding the commencement of this case to a self-settled trust or similar device of which the debtor is a beneficiary.

NAME OF TRUST OR OTHER DEVICE	DATE(S) OF TRANSFER(S)	AMOUNT OF MONEY OR DESCRIPTION AND VALUE OF PROPERTY OR DEBTOR'S INTEREST IN PROPERTY

11. Closed financial accounts

None
☐

List all financial accounts and instruments held in the name of the debtor or for the benefit of the debtor which were closed, sold, or otherwise transferred within **one year** immediately preceding the commencement of this case. Include checking, savings, or other financial accounts, certificates of deposit, or other instruments; shares and share accounts held in banks, credit unions, pension funds, cooperatives, associations, brokerage houses and other financial institutions. (Married debtors filing under chapter 12 or chapter 13 must include information concerning accounts or instruments held by or for either or both spouses whether or not a joint petition is filed, unless the spouses are separated and a joint petition is not filed.)

NAME AND ADDRESS OF INSTITUTION	TYPE OF ACCOUNT, LAST FOUR DIGITS OF ACCOUNT NUMBER, AND AMOUNT OF FINAL BALANCE	AMOUNT AND DATE OF SALE OR CLOSING

6

12. Safe deposit boxes

None ☐   List each safe deposit or other box or depository in which the debtor has or had securities, cash, or other valuables within **one year** immediately preceding the commencement of this case. (Married debtors filing under chapter 12 or chapter 13 must include boxes or depositories of either or both spouses whether or not a joint petition is filed, unless the spouses are separated and a joint petition is not filed.)

NAME AND ADDRESS OF BANK OR OTHER DEPOSITORY	NAMES AND ADDRESSES OF THOSE WITH ACCESS TO BOX OR DEPOSITORY	DESCRIPTION OF CONTENTS	DATE OF TRANSFER OR SURRENDER, IF ANY

---

13. Setoffs

None ☐   List all setoffs made by any creditor, including a bank, against a debt or deposit of the debtor within 90 days preceding the commencement of this case. (Married debtors filing under chapter 12 or chapter 13 must include information concerning either or both spouses whether or not a joint petition is filed, unless the spouses are separated and a joint petition is not filed.)

NAME AND ADDRESS OF CREDITOR	DATE OF SETOFF	AMOUNT OF SETOFF

---

14. Property held for another person

None ☐   List all property owned by another person that the debtor holds or controls.

NAME AND ADDRESS OF OWNER	DESCRIPTION AND VALUE OF PROPERTY	LOCATION OF PROPERTY

---

15. Prior address of debtor

None ☐   If debtor has moved within three years immediately preceding the commencement of this case, list all premises which the debtor occupied during that period and vacated prior to the commencement of this case. If a joint petition is filed, report also any separate address of either spouse.

ADDRESS	NAME USED	DATES OF OCCUPANCY

---

16. Spouses and Former Spouses

None
☐

If the debtor resides or resided in a community property state, commonwealth, or territory (including Alaska, Arizona, California, Idaho, Louisiana, Nevada, New Mexico, Puerto Rico, Texas, Washington, or Wisconsin) within eight years immediately preceding the commencement of the case, identify the name of the debtor's spouse and of any former spouse who resides or resided with the debtor in the community property state.

NAME

---

17. Environmental Information.

For the purpose of this question, the following definitions apply:

"Environmental Law" means any federal, state, or local statute or regulation regulating pollution, contamination, releases of hazardous or toxic substances, wastes or material into the air, land, soil, surface water, groundwater, or other medium, including, but not limited to, statutes or regulations regulating the cleanup of these substances, wastes, or material.

"Site" means any location, facility, or property as defined under any Environmental Law, whether or not presently or formerly owned or operated by the debtor, including, but not limited to, disposal sites.

"Hazardous Material" means anything defined as a hazardous waste, hazardous substance, toxic substance, hazardous material, pollutant, or contaminant or similar term under an Environmental Law.

None
☐

a. List the name and address of every site for which the debtor has received notice in writing by a governmental unit that it may be liable or potentially liable under or in violation of an Environmental Law. Indicate the governmental unit, the date of the notice, and, if known, the Environmental Law:

SITE NAME AND ADDRESS	NAME AND ADDRESS OF GOVERNMENTAL UNIT	DATE OF NOTICE	ENVIRONMENTAL LAW

None
☐

b. List the name and address of every site for which the debtor provided notice to a governmental unit of a release of Hazardous Material. Indicate the governmental unit to which the notice was sent and the date of the notice.

SITE NAME AND ADDRESS	NAME AND ADDRESS OF GOVERNMENTAL UNIT	DATE OF NOTICE	ENVIRONMENTAL LAW

None
☐

c. List all judicial or administrative proceedings, including settlements or orders, under any Environmental Law with respect to which the debtor is or was a party. Indicate the name and address of the governmental unit that is or was a party to the proceeding, and the docket number.

NAME AND ADDRESS OF GOVERNMENTAL UNIT	DOCKET NUMBER	STATUS OR DISPOSITION

---

18. Nature, location and name of business

None
☐

a. *If the debtor is an individual,* list the names, addresses, taxpayer-identification numbers, nature of the businesses, and beginning and ending dates of all businesses in which the debtor was an officer, director, partner, or managing executive of a corporation, partner in a partnership, sole proprietor, or was self-employed in a trade, profession, or other activity either full- or part-time within **six years** immediately preceding the commencement of this case, or in which the debtor owned 5 percent or more of the voting or equity securities within **six years** immediately preceding the commencement of this case.

If the debtor is a partnership, list the names, addresses, taxpayer-identification numbers, nature of the businesses, and beginning and ending dates of all businesses in which the debtor was a partner or owned 5 percent or more of the voting or equity securities, within **six years** immediately preceding the commencement of this case.

If the debtor is a corporation, list the names, addresses, taxpayer-identification numbers, nature of the businesses, and beginning and ending dates of all businesses in which the debtor was a partner or owned 5 percent or more of the voting or equity securities within **six years** immediately preceding the commencement of this case.

NAME	LAST FOUR DIGITS OF SOCIAL-SECURITY OR OTHER INDIVIDUAL TAXPAYER-I.D. NO. (ITIN) COMPLETE EIN	ADDRESS	NATURE OF BUSINESS	BEGINNING AND ENDING DATES

None ☐   b. Identify any business listed in response to subdivision a., above, that is "single asset real estate" as defined in 11 U.S.C. § 101.

      NAME   ADDRESS

The following questions are to be completed by every debtor that is a corporation or partnership and by any individual debtor who is or has been, within **six years** immediately preceding the commencement of this case, any of the following: an officer, director, managing executive, or owner of more than 5 percent of the voting or equity securities of a corporation; a partner, other than a limited partner, of a partnership; a sole proprietor, or self-employed in a trade, profession, or other activity, either full- or part-time.

*(An individual or joint debtor should complete this portion of the statement **only** if the debtor is or has been in business, as defined above, within six years immediately preceding the commencement of this case. A debtor who has not been in business within those six years should go directly to the signature page.)*

---

19. Books, records and financial statements

None ☐   a. List all bookkeepers and accountants who within **two years** immediately preceding the filing of this bankruptcy case kept or supervised the keeping of books of account and records of the debtor.

      NAME AND ADDRESS   DATES SERVICES RENDERED

None ☐   b. List all firms or individuals who within **two years** immediately preceding the filing of this bankruptcy case have audited the books of account and records, or prepared a financial statement of the debtor.

      NAME   ADDRESS   DATES SERVICES RENDERED

Appendices

9

None ☐   c. List all firms or individuals who at the time of the commencement of this case were in possession of the books of account and records of the debtor. If any of the books of account and records are not available, explain.

        NAME   ADDRESS

None ☐   d. List all financial institutions, creditors and other parties, including mercantile and trade agencies, to whom a financial statement was issued by the debtor within **two years** immediately preceding the commencement of this case.

        NAME AND ADDRESS   DATE ISSUED

20. Inventories

None ☐   a. List the dates of the last two inventories taken of your property, the name of the person who supervised the taking of each inventory, and the dollar amount and basis of each inventory.

DOLLAR AMOUNT
OF INVENTORY
DATE OF INVENTORY   INVENTORY SUPERVISOR   (Specify cost, market or other basis)

None ☐   b. List the name and address of the person having possession of the records of each of the inventories reported in a.. above.

                                               NAME AND ADDRESSES
                                               OF CUSTODIAN
DATE OF INVENTORY   OF INVENTORY RECORDS

21. Current Partners, Officers, Directors and Shareholders

None ☐   a. If the debtor is a partnership, list the nature and percentage of partnership interest of each member of the partnership.

NAME AND ADDRESS   NATURE OF INTEREST   PERCENTAGE OF INTEREST

None ☐   b. If the debtor is a corporation, list all officers and directors of the corporation, and each stockholder who directly or indirectly owns, controls, or holds 5 percent or more of the voting or equity securities of the corporation.

                                         NATURE AND PERCENTAGE
NAME AND ADDRESS   TITLE   OF STOCK OWNERSHIP

10

22 . Former partners. officers, directors and shareholders

None ☐   a.   If the debtor is a partnership, list each member who withdrew from the partnership within **one year** immediately preceding the commencement of this case.

NAME   ADDRESS   DATE OF WITHDRAWAL

None ☐   b.   If the debtor is a corporation, list all officers or directors whose relationship with the corporation terminated within **one year** immediately preceding the commencement of this case.

NAME AND ADDRESS   TITLE   DATE OF TERMINATION

---

23 . Withdrawals from a partnership or distributions by a corporation

None ☐   If the debtor is a partnership or corporation, list all withdrawals or distributions credited or given to an insider, including compensation in any form, bonuses, loans, stock redemptions, options exercised and any other perquisite during **one year** immediately preceding the commencement of this case.

NAME & ADDRESS OF RECIPIENT. RELATIONSHIP TO DEBTOR	DATE AND PURPOSE OF WITHDRAWAL	AMOUNT OF MONEY OR DESCRIPTION AND VALUE OF PROPERTY

---

24. Tax Consolidation Group.

None ☐   If the debtor is a corporation, list the name and federal taxpayer-identification number of the parent corporation of any consolidated group for tax purposes of which the debtor has been a member at any time within **six years** immediately preceding the commencement of the case.

NAME OF PARENT CORPORATION   TAXPAYER-IDENTIFICATION NUMBER (EIN)

---

25. Pension Funds.

None ☐   If the debtor is not an individual, list the name and federal taxpayer-identification number of any pension fund to which the debtor, as an employer, has been responsible for contributing at any time within **six years** immediately preceding the commencement of the case.

NAME OF PENSION FUND   TAXPAYER-IDENTIFICATION NUMBER (EIN)

* * * * * *

[If completed by an individual or individual and spouse]

I declare under penalty of perjury that I have read the answers contained in the foregoing statement of financial affairs and any attachments thereto and that they are true and correct.

Date _____

Signature
of Debtor _____

Date _____

Signature of
Joint Debtor
(if any) _____

[If completed on behalf of a partnership or corporation]

I declare under penalty of perjury that I have read the answers contained in the foregoing statement of financial affairs and any attachments thereto and that they are true and correct to the best of my knowledge, information and belief.

Date _____

Signature _____

Print Name and
Title _____

[An individual signing on behalf of a partnership or corporation must indicate position or relationship to debtor.]

___continuation sheets attached

Penalty for making a false statement. Fine of up to $500,000 or imprisonment for up to 5 years, or both. 18 U.S.C. §§ 152 and 3571

DECLARATION AND SIGNATURE OF NON-ATTORNEY BANKRUPTCY PETITION PREPARER (See 11 U.S.C. § 110)

I declare under penalty of perjury that: (1) I am a bankruptcy petition preparer as defined in 11 U.S.C. § 110; (2) I prepared this document for compensation and have provided the debtor with a copy of this document and the notices and information required under 11 U.S.C. §§ 110(b), 110(h), and 342(b); and, (3) if rules or guidelines have been promulgated pursuant to 11 U.S.C. § 110(h) setting a maximum fee for services chargeable by bankruptcy petition preparers, I have given the debtor notice of the maximum amount before preparing any document for filing for a debtor or accepting any fee from the debtor, as required by that section.

Printed or Typed Name and Title, if any, of Bankruptcy Petition Preparer   Social-Security No. (Required by 11 U.S.C. § 110.)

If the bankruptcy petition preparer is not an individual, state the name, title (if any), address, and social-security number of the officer, principal, responsible person, or partner who signs this document.

Address

Signature of Bankruptcy Petition Preparer   Date

Names and Social-Security numbers of all other individuals who prepared or assisted in preparing this document unless the bankruptcy petition preparer is not an individual:

If more than one person prepared this document, attach additional signed sheets conforming to the appropriate Official Form for each person

A bankruptcy petition preparer's failure to comply with the provisions of title 11 and the Federal Rules of Bankruptcy Procedure may result in fines or imprisonment or both. 18 U.S.C. § 156.

ABOUT THE AUTHOR

Christopher M. Kennedy is a partner in the law firm of Kennedy & Kennedy in Mankato, Minnesota. He practices in the area of financial law with a focus on consumer bankruptcies. He frequently assists individuals and small businesses with their financial concerns. He is happily married and enjoys time with his wife, Michele, and their three children.

ASPATORE